Materializing Fairness

Applied Gender Studies

edited by the

Gender and Women's Research Centre of the
Hessian Universities of Applied Sciences

Volume 9

Geschlechterforschung für die Praxis

herausgegeben vom

Gender- und Frauenforschungszentrum
der Hessischen Hochschulen (gFFZ)

Band 9

Julia-Constance Dissel
Melanie Levick-Parkin (eds.)

Materializing Fairness

Addressing Gender in Design and Tech

Verlag Barbara Budrich
Opladen • Berlin • Toronto 2025

All rights reserved. No part of this publication may be reproduced, stored in or introduced into a retrieval system, or transmitted, in any form, or by any means (electronic, mechanical, photocopying, recording or otherwise) without the prior written permission of Verlag Barbara Budrich. Any person who does any unauthorized act in relation to this publication may be liable to criminal prosecution and civil claims for damages.

You must not circulate this book in any other binding or cover and you must impose this same condition on any acquirer.

A CIP catalogue record for this book is available from
Die Deutsche Nationalbibliothek (The German National Library):
https://portal.dnb.de.

The contributions in this book were assessed in a double-blind peer review.

Carbon compensated production

© 2025 by Verlag Barbara Budrich GmbH, Opladen, Berlin & Toronto

    ISBN   978-3-8474-3108-4 (Paperback)
    eISBN   978-3-8474-3243-2 (PDF)
    DOI   10.3224/84743108

Verlag Barbara Budrich GmbH
Stauffenbergstr. 7. D-51379 Leverkusen Opladen, Germany |
info@budrich.de | www.budrich.de

86 Delma Drive. Toronto, ON M8W 4P6 Canada | info@budrich.de |
www.budrich.eu

Cover design by Bettina Lehfeldt, Kleinmachnow – www.lehfeldtgraphic.de
Typesetting by Linda Kutzki, Berlin – www.textsalz.de
Printed in Europe on FSC®-certified paper by Libri Plureos, Hamburg

Table of Content

Introduction. On Purpose, Tools and Projects: Feeding into
Sustainable Development Goals 5 & 10 7
Julia-Constance Dissel & Melanie Levick-Parkin

Ecofeminism. How Our System Is Devouring Nature, Labor, and Care, –
and What Design Can Do about it 15
Christian Bauer

An Intersectional Design Approach to Sustainable and Inclusive Futures 35
Hannah Jones and Londa Schiebinger

Materialising gender fairness through iconic language: empowering tools from
and for the design community 51
Valeria Bucchetti and Fransesca Casnati

Why Representation Matters: Reclaiming Space – The Evolution of Women in Tech 65
Franziska Beckert

Idle Uses and Body Comfort: Redesigning the Campus of the largest
University in Argentina 75
Griselda Flesler and Carolina Spataro

Involve and intervene 93
Julia Pierzina

Glossary 105
Index 109
Authors 111

Introduction
On Purpose, Tools and Projects: Feeding into Sustainable Development Goals 5 & 10

Julia-Constance Dissel & Melanie Levick-Parkin

Materialising Fairness presents body of work which aims to draw together the topics of 'fairness – gender – design and tech'. With it, we gratefully build on traditions of feminist critiques of design and the relatively young discipline of design philosophy, as well as the very lively contemporary discussions around gender and design, decolonising design and ontological design, amongst others. The volume draws on a small selection of very diverse accounts of practitioners and scholars from Design and Tech, who are engaged with projects that have gender and fairness as a central focus.

As editors we very much value theoretical and rhetorical discussions around gender issues in design and tech, but the goal of this volume is to also provide readers, specifically students, teachers and practitioners, with methods, tools and input from real world and academic projects as well as the lived experiences that accompanies them, so that they may practically guide the readers towards targeted reflection and action relevant to their own settings. We acknowledge that our world is in crisis and that the path to sustainability is formed by many factors, – gender equality being just one important aspect. We do, however, come from a position that sees gender injustices as intrinsically linked to patriarchal and capitalist mechanisms of environmental exploitation and degradation which are deeply connected through inseparable intersectional categories of social exclusion. In line with this conviction the book centres on issues around gender injustice, with a focus on instruments and project reports as well as individual experiences, so that readers interested in aspects of diversity, intersectionality and gender can harness some practical tools that might help them achieve better gender equality outcomes in their work and lives, whilst also building empathy with others. However, as it is relevant to convey the complexity of concepts and questions surrounding any gender projects today – specifically referring to injustice and the interrelationships between social (gender), ecological and economic factors – we are intentionally opening this book with a relatively theory-laden contribution, that prepares the reader conceptually and critically by providing them with a broader historical and scientific background of feminist thought against which fair and inclusive design has to position itself today.

We also feel compelled to give a little more detail on the overall philosophical framework in which this volume is embedded within this introduction. As design philosophers and design educators, we are acutely aware that everything within the human mantle is designed, – from the chairs we sit on, to the cities we live in, to the systems that govern us, even many aspects of ourselves as social beings. Nature has largely been co-opted into human culture as an assumed neutral resource pit to be exploited as we see fit and just like the rest of the world, design is becoming more and more driven by (digital) technology. Therefore, it is not enough to talk about design only in terms of product or communication design, there is a steady convergence of classic design tasks and research and technical application areas. But from an *observing philosophical standpoint* everything we do, – every creational act, in (technological) design, is an act with moral implication. This is because the results of the actions taken, or the impact of the creations themselves, will inevitably be more or less *right* or *wrong*, in the sense that they contribute *positively* or *negatively* to – peoples' wellbeing, – or that of nature, – or the stability of a society, for example. Whether something is considered *right* or *wrong* is not a neutral judgement but is bound by the ethics and positionality of the judging criterion.

In everyday life, it can often be difficult to take full account of being a moral and specifically fair agent, – to be reflexive of the fact that the things we do have often complex moral dimensions and implications. It can be even more challenging to acknowledge and reflect on this predicament when we are acting in roles bestowed on us due to our training as designers or technologists. Because roles by their nature are to be fulfilled within certain parameters usually not determined by us, and within that there is the potential to not only loose a sense of individual agency, but also to feel relieved of a certain amount of responsibility for our actions whilst in this role. With this book we aim to remind ourselves and to inspire anyone else charged with designing at any scale, to consider that, what we do (or don't do) always has moral implications and that the labour spent to attend to the moral dimensions of our work, does help and is worthwhile, – even if the scale of the task often appears unsurmountable and its baby steps all the way at best. We would specifically like to call to action an enhanced awareness of the way in which gender shapes the design of systems and artefacts and how a lack of having specifiers for ethical, fair behaviour that takes account of these gender dimensions, means an unconscious perpetual re-production of harmful and exclusionary practices solidified in our still mostly man-made environments at the expense of the natural world of which we are part of.

Since it can be difficult to situate oneself definitively within complex and tricky ethical frameworks, it can be helpful to build on existing frameworks that are already being tested and probed in the light of day through the labour of many others. To this extend, the moral framework we are setting out from is ultimately reflected in the SDGs formulated by the UN, specifically calling on SDG number 5 and 10, insofar in one way or another, all contributions of this book pursue to counteract discrimination based on gender through special design interventions and reflections. This includes women and girls but ultimately refers to all forms of gender discrimination and therefore to all human beings. Design in this book is hereby understood as the means and tools to implement and materialise justice and equality, by counteracting biases and disadvantages people experience in the workplace and in their lives. This is a task the SDGs due to their abstract nature do not provide precise guidance on. However, we also want to place a slightly different emphasis on commitments to morality and sustainability. In this context we opt for the concept of *fairness* rather than for *equality*. Within larger contexts, such as at institutional levels, the idea of equality, equal access and opportunities and thus issues of parity, quite rightly play a major role in gender issues pertinent within the UN framework.

There are however further dimensions to the gender injustices that shape our everyday lives and society as a whole, and it is those we aim to shine further light onto. The concept of fairness is pivotal to those dimensions, because general ideas of justice and equality expressed as universal rules can be limiting when it comes to weighing up full impact of the complexities and intricacies when imbalances and biases play out. In order to navigate through these deep social waters successfully, it helps to consider values such as reasonableness, decency, empathy, and fair treatment rather than just to agree to the sheer compliance with (moral) rules of justice and equality.

We have to acknowledge that people in their roles as designers or engineers or just as consumers often make decisions on the basis of socio-cultural mechanisms they are often not even aware of; – due to tradition, – for the sake of time and energy efficiency, – and of course also out of comfort, humans often act according to taste and habit, both of which are mostly very unreflective companions in our lives. And when we are dealing with gender issues, we are not just talking about equal numbers and equal access to opportunities, we are talking about the hidden, often false and misguided, expectations and ideas about people's supposed dispositions, abilities and incapacities that are incorporated into these habits of thought. As designers we might consider these as 'design scripts' that live in our heads, as much as in our actions, environments and artefacts, and they are passed down to us by our culture, traditions and training. It seems only natural that without conscious intervention, the drivers of design and also (digital) technology, like AI or coding, reproduce existing problematic societal patterns, including inequality, unfairness, restrictions and narrowness of many complex kind. We don't see this primarily as the moral failure of the individual who is designing any particular aspect within our systems, but as a logical consequence of our world being dominated by a patriarchal capitalist system that is built on very narrow normative stereotypes and biases, resistant to change of the norm and traditions that benefit few while exploiting the rest, not just in relation to gender. When we finally arrive at the question as to how to start to disentangle and dismantle such strait jackets of thought and action, and how to materialise change through the creation of different 'design scripts' within the tangible and intangible world, we arrive back at the idea of ontology. Design is what we think *it is*, what we agree on *it is*, what we make it *to be*. This means we can, at any given point, change its very nature and the parameters of what its goals should be.

So, we will start back at the beginning, which is to remind ourselves that – what we think, is what we design, and – what we design, is what shapes us back. So, the task is always twofold in every respect. The challenge is to remain alert to our own agency to critically evaluate the traditional structures we are situated within, to dismantle those that don't serve us and to design the tools to create new ones that do.

Framing the complexity of these challenges, Christian Bauer's focus on Ecofeminism and Design seems to be a good starting point for this book. He begins with critical and historical insights into Rawl's 'theory of justice as fairness', also tapping into the idea of intertemporal justice echoed in the sustainable development goals whilst taking account of the need to attend to more-than-human ontologies in design. As he explains, we can no longer ignore how our patriarchal capitalist system is devouring labour, nature and care, and how design as a discipline has been historically a great facilitator of this destruction and continues to be complicit in systems that lead us towards social and environmental dead points. His appeal to designers, – to consider other roles that design can inhabit by taking up the resistance stance that underlies the utopian justice ideas of ecofeminist criticism, is a timely one. He proposes that Ecofeminism does not only present an excellent framework for an intellectual and activist resistance movement in general, but because of its concern with materiality lends itself to be a catalyst for a reflective and reflexive design practice of the future. As an activist stance and as a philosophy, ecofeminism has been lived and re-enlivened by many women from around the world, particularly from the global south. It has also become a broad church for those of any gender identity who have identified the structures of heteropatriarchal capitalism as being central to their own oppression and intrinsically connected to the exploitation of nature. Since this takes shape as crimes against both humanity and against the dignity of Mother Earth, Bauer highlights ecofeminist approaches as a pertinent starting point of a resistance movement for designers, one which emphasizes the relevance of designers awakening in order to escape the clutches of an outdated design system and making values such as sustainability and fairness central goals within what we understand of as 'design'.

The second contribution, by Hannah Jones and Londa Schiebinger, concretely shows what a critical evaluation of our design tools to enable the materialisation of more just and fair outcomes, can actually look like. This second chapter showcases their *Intersectional Design Cards – a collaborative tool developed to support teams in creating radically inclusive products, processes and paradigms*, this equity-based design toolkit offers up concrete design instruments to be used during the design process to take account of gendered and specifically intersectional innovation. Motivated by the idea of tackling social and environmental inequities, specifically in the realm of emerging technologies, this chapter discusses some of the ways in which design has failed in terms of fairness and where/how design can find new opportunities for achieving greater sustainability in terms of society and planet. The discussion includes a review of outcomes when the cards were used in prior trials with students and professionals in the design industry, including from the 'Innovations in Inclusive Design' class at the Hasso Plattner Institute of Design (d.school), Stanford University, US, to inform the creation of intersectional design concepts. As an applied and well-designed toolkit-based intervention, this contribution is both practical and accessible, whilst starting to show how concepts of fairness might be materialised during the design process.

The next article by Valeria Bucchetti, and Fransesca Casnati also deals with the provision and development of tools and highlights the importance of recognising the gendered nature of visual language, ultimately entailing a manifesto for gender sensitive communication in and through design. While the second contribution can basically be understood as an innovation tool in a broader context, applicable for and in multiple design and technological such as engineering situations, this third contribution focuses primarily on the topic of iconic language and thus on empowering tools that need to be reflected on in the context of communication design. At the heart of this lies a critical examination of the domain of visual representation and iconic languages as a possible vehicle of gender representations that can shape individual and collective biographies in both positive and negative ways. It expands to the Manifesto that is meant as an instrument for self-reflection and concrete guidance in daily design practice, supplemented by strategies to bypass stereotypes and clichés and to transform the effects of representations.

In the next article by Franziska Beckert, scientific research and personal lived experience are drawn on together to give lively account of how the problematics of gender inequality materialise in the tech sector. It takes stock of the subordinate role that women continue to play today in the tech industry, despite their influential roles in the histories of tech development. It goes on to highlight how these inequalities and injustices based on gender impact on the development of innovative solutions and lead to the reproduction of stereotypical background assumptions which in turn help perpetuate these inequalities and misrepresentations. Critically, the author does not only question the causes of these unfairness's theoretically but also maps out opportunities for practical transformations that offers a gender-just perspective on the future of programming, making it clear why this matters for all of us.

The last two chapters of this volume are dedicated to projects that although they have been developed within and for educational contexts, they offer much wider potential for application and a much more broadly relevant critique. Both projects are of an exploratory nature that takes account of the difficulty to pinpoint issues of gender within the tangible and intangible of system. Viewed through a feminist lens it becomes clear that the intangible nature of emotions and embodied knowledge we all carry, must be taken into account in any teaching or educational environment before we can attend to any material changes identified as necessary to further gender equality.

In Griselda Flesner's and Cardna Spartano's account of the re-design of campus space at the University of Buenos Aires Campus, the intangible and embodied desires and demands of students and teachers regarding the need for places for leisure and rest are examined. A feminist lens informs the methodology used to examine new ways of assessing human need on a campus that was designed with the functionalist criteria of the Modern Movement. This highlights that in order to create holistic, human scale environments for study and work, demands for other 'non-productive' uses need to be met. Based on a survey conducted in 2020 that investigated the sensations generated by different spaces on the Campus, the authors' focus demands for an architecture that is sensitive to the needs of the body which are not to be separated from the needs of the mind. This space is opened up by students participating FADU's seminar 'Design and Gender Studies', whose critical design approaches highlight that modernism is a social construct in need of critique by exploring opportunities for the design of university spaces that takes account of the way in which fairness, as an intangible design parameter, can nevertheless be materialised.

Our last contribution by Julia Pierzina takes up a transdisciplinary approach, which is design research led and strongly informed by social sciences, in order to investigate how perceptions of social structures bring gendered norms into being. It acts as a project report as well as a plea to intervene and interfere based on the authors own approach of an *inverse artefact analysis*. The research finds that imitation and an unquestioning stance in relation to lived gender-specific attributions have a far greater impact on the reality of young pupils than for example abstract laws of equality. Thus, the author highlights that problematic gender scripts in the social realm are major factors in need of being tackled by design, and that this must include the material *and* immaterial dimensions of our social environments. Traditionally design centred on the materialisation of artefacts and investigates their material dimensions in order to inform better design solutions, but the author points to the importance of paying attention to the social realm in which such artefacts are handled and being materialised through often gendered presumptions. Inverse artefact analysis presents itself as a productive method or tool, to not only recognise existing structures and understanding patterns and intervening from within by questioning and criticising them, but also to possibly recognise them as an intervention designer. It is all about discovering the subliminal nuances to materialise fairness out of what is immaterialised in our social worlds.

We hope this volume will inspire people in academic and non-academic contexts to make use of the many opportunities and instruments that design gives us to make our world a more inclusive and fairer place and we also hope that through this publication all readers will realise that the question of how we shape our world is not in the hands of designers alone, but requires an alignment of designers and consumers/clients/people in general with the will to together shape the world for the better. We would like to express our sincere thanks to all the contributors to this volume, not least because the development had to go through many loops and during this process and the foregone research on initiatives it became clear that the efforts put into the topic of gender fairness, particularly in the academic design context and in professional practice, urgently need to be expanded. In this sense, the contributions from individuals and initiatives selected here also serve as beacons that are worth focusing on to inform a better future as we envision it within and beyond the framework of the UN-sustainable development goals aiming to further gender justice. Finally, it is important to us to point out that design today cannot do without an interdisciplinary and transdisciplinary perspective. The design expertise of the authors gathered in this book has been informed by a range of different scientific disciplines, their different regional origins also inspired their specific approaches and diverse styles of representation. For us as editors, this collection is an intentional act also reflecting a challenge of our time, namely to process the diversity of science, regions and life in general to be valued and appreciated within the design practice itself.

Ecofeminism. How Our System Is Devouring Nature, Labor, and Care, – and What Design Can Do about it

Christian Bauer

1 John Rawls' idea of fairness and the ecofeminist concept of justice

Imagine we lived in a world in which everyone had equal starting conditions. This could be described as having equal opportunity. Now, imagine we lived in a world in which all people had secure access to clean drinking water, to shelter that offered protection from climate events, and to a healthy diet. This could be called resource justice. For some, this world is within reach, for others, light-years away. This is what we call social injustice.

The American political philosopher and theorist John Rawls' (1921–2002) theory of 'justice as fairness', could be considered a pivotal anchor point for this anthology. This particular contribution aligns itself with the central theme of 'Materialising Fairness – Addressing Gender in Design & Tech' by adopting an anti-patriarchal position which is critical of technology and capitalism, inspired and informed by ecofeminist critique and philosophy. Before taking a closer look at the various manifestations of ecofeminism and clarifying its relevance, we will briefly recall the impact of the powerful horizon of justice which Rawls established through his work.

'Justice as Fairness – a Restatement' (2001) presents an evolution of Rawls' political concepts which he first established in works such as 'A Theory of Justice' (1971), 'Political Liberalism'(1999), and 'The Law of Peoples' (1999). Förster highlights that "Justice as Fairness' focuses on Rawls' conception of basic justice in a well-ordered basic structure of a liberal democracy' (ibid. 2023: 63). "With his contractarian theory of justice he is methodologically in pursuit of an individualistic project, with the intent to facilitate a reason-oriented pluralism. He envisions a free society where free and equal individuals have agency, and (should) ideally make use of their freedom in a way that is oriented towards the common good. In contrast to this, experience tells us that most people only have access to a very limited version of this freedom.

Is the world and society therefore unjust? From a strictly egalitarian perspective, this is probably the case. But Rawls himself does not advocate strict or idealistic egalitarianism. He's too liberal for that. He clearly recognises that many social inequalities exist. But in his opinion, not all inequalities are to be regarded as unjust. Certain inequalities are to be tolerated on the condition that 'they work to everyone's advantage' (Rawls 2020: 13). Rawls calls this the 'Difference Principle'.

With his concepts in 'Justice as Fairness', Rawls stands on the always shaky ground of liberalism. Although a political theory with a venerable tradition, its ground is always shaky because its basic political, philosophical and economic unit is that of the bourgeois individual. And, this individual is fickle. It therefore makes sense for Rawls to abandon an overly individualistic position right at the beginning of his reflections. He claims that he understands justice 'exclusively as a virtue of social institutions or in the context of what I will call practices' (Rawls 2020: 9). By referring to the virtues, he builds a hinge into his theory that can function both as a supra-personal horizon of social determinations and as an emotional motivator for individual actions of all kinds. By referring to the practices of justice, by bringing up the 'system of rules' that is omnipresent in our everyday lives, be it in 'court hearings and parliaments', be it when we think of 'markets and property systems' (ibid.: 9, footnote 2), he sets an interesting accent that leads us to the practices of design.

We may not always reflect on this, but design is a highly rule-based discipline. Many advocates like to give design the appearance of an undisciplined discipline (Kaiser / Stephany 2021). However, this view obscures the extent to which modern design owes itself to scientific and technological progress and the functionalist categories of an utilitarian modernity. However, the nature of progress and the general orientation towards utility mean that their discrete charm cannot unfold equally everywhere. The development of scientific, technological and media possibilities takes place in different parts of the world in different societies in a non-simultaneity of simultaneity. This is not always fair. Development and the associated economic growth also raise questions of environmental ethics, which Rawls did not address in detail throughout his life. In order to find out what fairness theoretically consists of and what it achieves (in terms of impartiality), Rawls developed the "veil of ignorance" method. This is a famous thought experiment that Rawls devised to illustrate his concept of justice: The central idea is that the position an individual takes to a question of fairness when they are ignorant of/have no stake in the social setting and structure of an issue, should be considered as impartial. He conceived this position as a moral standpoint at a time when the environmental movement in the USA was already sending out clear warning signals and the Club of Rome report "Limits to Growth" (1972) was on everyone's lips. The fact that the state was urged by environmental activists to take precautions against environmental disasters of biblical proportions could only be missed by an academic of his stature under the veil of deliberate ignorance. However, environmental ethical questions such as 'intertemporal justice' actually only play a minimal role for Rawls insofar as they cannot be represented and dealt with through his 'principle of freedom and difference' (Ekardt / Winter 2023: 623, author's translation).

But the negative consequences on the lives, health and livelihoods of countless people whose lives are being destroyed by the fossil oil industries' pyrotechnics is a persistent problem. The pyrotechnic furor of the fossil fuel industry presents a persistent disruptive factor in relation to issues of justice globally, as it destroys the health, livelihoods and lives of countless people worldwide. It negatively impacts on people's dignity around the world not only through the burning of coal, gas and oil, but also through the loss of biodiversity, the rampant degradation of soil, and the general contamination of water and air. All these horrendous losses, which are basically almost impossible to quantify, are hardly affected by Rawls' difference principle. Only his 'saving principle' might make people prefer sustainable and intergenerationally just economic activity. 'The saving principle is supposed to dictate that each generation should leave behind for the next exactly what it would have good reason to claim for itself (Rawls 1975: 319–327).' (ibid.: 623) Drawing on this, the international community has come at least this far by presenting the definition of sustainable development in the 1986 UN report "Our Common Future" (better known as the "Brundlandt Report"), which has been valid ever since and by which means current national practices are still coordinated under the auspices of the sustainable development goals.

In contrast to this, ecofeminist activists of recent decades, who today also act primarily as promoters of an ecofeminism that is 'intersectional, interdisciplinary and international' (Hansen / Gerner 2024: 17), do not shy back from emphasizing these concrete injustices and inequalities that prevail worldwide. In many cases, the injustices and violations of human dignity are directly or indirectly targeted against women and their children. These injustices are not atemporal – they enmesh the living and past generations, who, in the last centuries of technical-scientific development and economic growth, have left behind one thing above all: garbage and waste. Against the backdrop of litter pollution and the unresolved problems of 'final storage' which reveal a general lack of a 'will to sustainability' (Bauer 2024: 23–26), the question arises as to whether the members of contemporary societies should be regarded from the outset as the relatively privileged ones who have been particularly blessed by modern developments. The discourse on ecofeminist positions outlined below illustrates that the most advanced positions in applied sciences are not necessarily those that lead to a good, just and livable society. Incidentally, it was not Rawls' intention to theoretically enable such a society with his theory of justice. Rather, he made a restrictive statement: 'Justice should not be confused with a comprehensive view of a good society; it is only one part of any such conception. It is important, for example, to distinguish the sense of equality that is one aspect of the concept of justice from the sense of equality that is part of a broader ideal of society.' (Rawls 2020: 11)

In doing so, he cleverly salvages himself from claims that we will deal with below – the claims that arise from an ecofeminist reading of equality. The extent to which ecofeminists also intend a comprehensive social ideal will be discussed again in section three, when we take a closer look at the utopian potential of this intellectual and activist movement.

2 Sources and basic ideas of ecofeminism

2.1 Early birds, feminist collectives and protest movements

As the Australian sociologist Ariel Salleh explained in 'Ecofeminism as Politics. Nature, Marx, and the Postmodern', the beginnings of ecofeminism lie in the 'kitchens' of the 1960s in the USA, from which a veritable 'politicization of housework' was organized in the spirit of the fight against the nuclear industry and other technological threats, which led to the 'International Feminist Collective (IFK), a transnational network' (Hansen/Gerner 2024: 44f.). In this context, early forms of rebellion against classist, sexist and racist forms of oppression emerged, for which the term "intersectionality" exists since 1989 thanks to the lawyer Kimberlé Crenshaw. It is important to emphasise the simultaneity with which the politicisation of nature and the politicisation of domestic work came about.

Modern environmental awareness is significantly influenced by the reception of Rachel Carson's seminal work "The Silent Spring" (1962), which was the starting signal for environmental movements in the USA and worldwide. As a biologist, she linked the mass destruction of insects by the pesticide DDT with the mass extinction of other organisms such as birds and, not least, humans themselves. She thus elevated the consequences of extensive agriculture on the coexistence of micro- and macro-organisms to a broader political issue.

In various European countries such as Germany, Italy and France, feminist collectives emerged in the transition from the 1960s to the 1970s, campaigning against nuclear power and for peace. In France, Francoise d'Eaubonne published 'Feminism or Death. How the Women's Movement Can Save the Planet' (1974); many consider her being the originator of the term 'ecofeminism'. However, in addition to the anti-nuclear movements and parts of the peace movement, it is above all the activist groups outside Europe and North America that deserve attention. In these circles, an original ecofeminist critique of society was formulated, and it presents itself as a potent critique of the exploitation of nature and women, especially in the Global South.

Positions such as those of the sociologist Maria Mies (1931-2023) and the scientific theorist, social activist and winner of the Right Livelihood Award Vandana Shiva (*1952) make it clear that the female body is to be regarded as a colony of men. Shiva criticises the fact that the processes of colonization, which the Indian nation under Mahatma Gandhi and his successors successfully resisted, were seamlessly transformed after a few decades into international framework legislation such as GATT and the structural adjustment programmes (SAPs) of the IMF and the World Bank, which, under the title of "development", have led to the dispossession of the population and, in particular, of land-owning women.

The example of the 'Green Belt Movement' (GBM) in Kenya in turn teaches us how effective and sustainable female-inspired politics can be. This grassroots movement goes back to the initiative of the activist, PhD biologist and later Nobel Peace Prize winner Wangari Muta Maathai (1940-2011), thanks to whom "55 million trees have been planted" in recent decades, which has not only stopped the erosion of the soil, but has also been a 'pacifist and subversive act of re-empowerment and re-appropriation of their own livelihoods, a reclaiming of the forests by women' (Hansen / Gerner 2024: 52f.). Maathai became the first green politician in Africa to successfully combine the fight for women's rights with environmental protection. The GBM is still active today as an NGO and fights for climate adaptation strategies on the African continent.

2.2 Ecofeminist social critique

The ecofeminist critique of society as a critique of the exploitation of nature and women is intertwined with a general critique of *homo oeconomicus* as the predominant 'subject of economic theory' (Hansen / Gerner: 149f.) This criticism is often neo-Marxist in nature, as in the case of Maria Mies, Claudia von Werlhof (*1943) and Veronika Bennholdt-Thomsen (*1944), who, as representatives of the 'Bielefeld subsistence perspective', addressed the housewifeisation ('Hausfrauisierung') of women's contribution to working life: Processes of houswifeisation are accordingly those in which entire sectors of the population are forced to support economic development and the processes of capital accumulation through very cheap or even unpaid work, especially in the area of reproduction (von Werlhof/Mies/Bennholdt-Thomsen 1988: 66f.). Incidentally, housewifeisation is not limited to women. It also affects, for example, all those designers in the Western affluent zones who try to survive in precarious employment as "low-wage gender" (Claudia von Werlhof) in informal working conditions. More recently philosopher Nancy Fraser (*1947) has referred to the concept of housewifeisation in her study 'Cannibal Capitalism. How Our System Is Devouring Democracy, Care, and the Planet – and What We Can Do about it'. Fraser adopts Mies' position when she describes housewifeisation as the effect of 'liberal-colonial capitalism', which has manifested 'a new gender imaginary with separate spheres' of male-coded production and female-coded reproduction (Fraser 2023: 108). Long before Fraser, the 'Bielefeld women' combined a critical reading of Western development policy with a critique of growth and a critique of the material and social practices of the capitalist economy and form of society, in which many actors do not shy away from the greatest environmental disasters for the sake of profit. In her work 'Patriarchy & Capital' Mies emphasises this development right at the beginning:

'Between 1986 and today, the world situation has deteriorated overall. Natural and man-made disasters and crises have increased. Climate change, caused by our lifestyle, can no longer be reversed. The resources on whose exploitation our lifestyle is based are running out. The number of poor people has increased, not only in poor countries but also in rich ones. Nature is being destroyed more and more everywhere. In its greed for ever more profit, capitalism has no regard for people or nature. New technologies are invented to drive further growth, but all of them have a negative impact on people and nature.' (Mies 2015: 9, author's translation)

Even if this passage might make it seem so, ecofeminists are by no means doomsayers or prone to defeatism in the face of a dramatic planetary situation. Rather, they are genuine activists and courageous utopians who deal with the whole variety of violent state and private sector repression against marginalised interest groups such as indigenous populations, family and neighbourhood systems massively threatened by environmental damage, and who are constantly paving new paths towards citizenship undauntedly advocating a life of self-determination and maximum democracy for all genders.

2.3 Ecofeminist critique of science

Ecofeminist social critique is a critique of science that sometimes seamlessly merges into a critique of the positivist concept of science, which is partly responsible for bringing a mechanistic 'world view to the fields of women in the colonies' (Hansen/Gerner: 174f.). Carolyn Merchant (*1936) is one of the foremothers of this criticism. In her classic 'The Death of Nature. Women, Ecology, and the Scientific Revolution' (1980), she examines the period from 1500 to 1700 as the foremost relevant phase in which the formative approaches to our modern scientific concepts were developed. The modern founding fathers of the scientific revolution, such as Francis Bacon, Thomas Hobbes and René Descartes, brought about a fundamental change in cosmological ideas: Whereas the cosmos had been viewed as an organism since antiquity, this view changed radically from the 16th century onwards. The organism was replaced by the machine as the basic metaphor for the order of things. Since then, nothing fundamental has changed in this guiding concept. Only the various technological revolutions have broken down the images of the orderly whole into more and more individual elements. In this process of dissection, anatomy was a kind of guiding discipline in dealing with nature. Since the 16th century, both human and non-human nature has been cut up into smaller bits and pieces. Merchant therefore understands the course of modern science right up to the modern age as an unreserved denunciation of the bond between humans and nature. Nature, which has been appreciated as a nurturing mother and goddess (Ceres, Demeter, Gaia, Isis) since the ancient beginnings of Mediterranean and non-European civilizations, becomes an inanimate object during the scientific revolution – sheer matter without a soothing and life-giving force: 'The world we have lost was organic.' (Merchant 2020: 1). Philosopher Karen J. Warren (1947–2020), who created a foundational work with her volume 'Ecofeminist Philosophy: A Western Perspective on What It Is and Why It Matters' (2000), drew on such insights. In it, she makes it clear in all breadth and depth that the connections between feminism and environmental protection are 'historical (typically causal), conceptual, empirical, socioeconomic, linguistic, symbolic and literary, spiritual and religious, epistemological, political, and ethical' (Warren 2000: 21).

2.4 Ecofeminist critique of the concept of labour

'The worker can create nothing without nature' (Marx 2009: 85).

Part of the ecofeminist struggle is a critique of the prevailing concept of class and work. Beyond the problem of the 'housewifeisation' of working conditions recognized by the 'Bielefeld women', a positive concept of work for women was to be developed. The concept of work based on the political economy, anthropology and theory of alienation of the young Marx, with which the women's researcher Maria Mies comes up, is a critical corrective to short-sighted and abbreviated understandings of work. Work is generally understood as wage labour and employment that is traded on markets. The human worker sells their-self for a certain (lifetime) working time and in return receives the means to secure their livelihood. For many freelance creatives, this is in fact little more than the aforementioned means of subsistence and self-reproduction in their so-called leisure time, which primarily serves to restore their labour power. However, Marx's idea of labour does not only concern the dualism of labour time and leisure time, whereby the former is the tiresome, because necessary, labour time and the latter is the fun time, because it is allocated to the 'realm of freedom'. In Mies' reading, it is a matter of being 'on the way to a new society' (Mies 2015: 366f.) that involves saying goodbye to this dualistic model characterising both capitalism and socialism. Instead, we would be better off orienting ourselves towards forms of work that have a greater meaningfulness in themselves and that represent a life activity in the full sense, as the young Marx already believed when he emphatically wrote: 'But the productive life is the generic life. It is the life that generates life. The whole character of a species, its generic character, lies in the kind of life activity, and free conscious activity is the generic character of man.' (Marx 2009: 90, author's translation).

Similar to Marx, who understood work as the realization of essential human properties, whose negative counter-image is work characterised by alienation, we should, according to Mies, better reflect on forms of work that provide individual satisfaction through shared activities and the sensuality of this activities. Mies envisions the image of 'small farmers and craftsmen', where 'work can be understood as both a pleasure and a burden' (Mies 2016: 365, author's translation). Mies is looking for a positive concept of work, especially for women. It can be assumed or hoped that in the future, due to the dwindling supply of human resources on the labour market in the Global North, greater attention will be paid to the well-being of female employees. For some people, socio-ecological considerations are certainly playing an ever-greater role in their choice of employment than socio-economic issues. The growing number of city-quitters is a sign that people (have to) avoid the global pressure of exploitation in order not to unduly endanger their own physical and mental well-being. However, contrary to all the PR, country life is not a country lifestyle, but rather a question of organizing complex living and working contexts.

Meaning and sensuality are being lost in a technologically driven world of work that is becoming increasingly semi-automated. An ecofeminist concept of work, on the other hand, as envisioned by Mies, is oriented towards the human body and its social needs, which range from communication to 'erotic satisfaction' (Mies 2015: 367, author's translation). In the machine age, however, these human capacities are undermined by purely cognitive activities or negative emotions. Design, on the other hand, still includes certain material resources in order to maintain access to sensuality and the capacity for pleasure. However, such an approach presupposes that design is understood, taught and experimentally practiced primarily as an artistic discipline and not primarily as a media-technological one. If the future belongs to such sub-disciplines within design as human-machine interaction and interaction design with its mainly digitally operating tools, the channels for dealing with the environment will be reduced more and more to interfaces and mere simulations. A very limited set of sensorimotor skills is addressed at these user interfaces. Assuming that these interaction patterns are increasingly used to train generative AIs, it is to be expected that humans will provide a very limited picture of their best practices in their respective fields of action and work processes within AI-supported systems. Human environments are increasingly becoming robotic work envelopes. Generative AI is taking this image of humans into other contexts. In view of the already well-known racist and sexist attitudes of AIs, this is a frightening image because it is deeply discriminatory and affects gender roles (Constanza-Chock 2020). Here, design is not the art of the living, but merely the instrumental extension of the machine man.

Machines are a reflection of the reductionist understanding of science and the image of man that Merchant diagnosed in 'The Death of Nature'. In ecofeminist circles, the invasion of machines is understood as the colonisation of nature and women or female bodies in the name of patriarchy, the more recent varieties of which operate under the label 'petromasculinity' (Dagett 2024), among others. This concept refers to a historical development of male domination that makes use of an increasingly sprawling motorized machine park to cement power and violence relations. The political authoritarianism of our time, which is taking hold worldwide, is inconceivable without the increasingly aggressive intervention of machines as extensions of the alienated man. Yet the media and machine network systems are accepted willy-nilly and not identified as what they have long since have become: sacred instruments of the market economy, whose petromasculine representatives see themselves as entitled to inflict ever deeper injuries on the world. Petromasculinity is already destroying the biophysical foundations of democracy and freedom. Petromasculine machines transform natural resources into commodity forms. What is considered production under capitalism is in fact material destruction. Petromasculinity is therefore the natural enemy of climate protection and all those efforts of environmental and climate ethics that aim to mitigate foreseeable climate catastrophes. It is a problem creator that perfidiously sells itself not as a problem, but as part of the solution.

2.4 Ecofeminist Critique of Progressive Alienation and Technologisation

The colonisation of women under the auspices of science and biotechnology is another topic that ecofeminists are currently addressing with critical intent. From an ecofeminist perspective, the new reproductive technologies are part of a globally effective ideology of subjugating women wherever possible to the patriarchal-capitalist system of production, reproduction and exploitation. This ideology is particularly perfidious when it promotes medical technologies under the banner of emancipation, while these only serve to liberate women in a superficial sense and ultimately lead to self-alienation. Incidentally, the case of reproductive medicine to be discussed below perhaps even puts certain approaches of Western and contemporary design theory in a dubious light. This is because our customary design assumptions that so-called 'good design' has an emancipatory effect and, conversely, that non-emancipatory design cannot be good could, on closer inspection, be based on a dualistic short circuit (Bauer 2021: 59–78). Rather, it is the case that a design that seeks to reify simple gains in emancipation as an act of (even political) liberation falls short. Women's freedom is not simply to be had by design. It is not, if only because this design is usually an abstract-immaterial concept that corresponds to and exchange value, because women have to invest a lot of money in medical interventions. The question arises: What do women want with the blueprint of a genetically well-equipped designer baby: Is this her liberation when she gets a baby designed by specialists thanks to the latest reproductive and genetic technologies? Here too, the 'sexist and racist foundations' (Mies/Shiva 2016: 192f.) of the 21st century are embedded in the system of science and technology: Reproductive engineers offer a woman – in the name of her self-determination – what the ideal child should look like. They create a blueprint in the image of which the Promethean man breeds his (!) offspring – and creates people in his image (or in terms of population policy: according to his instructions).

Here, the entire sad history of contempt for women continues in the guise of science, which in past centuries led to the social or eugenic 'selection and elimination' (ibid., 194f.) of people. The female body becomes the raw material for the knowledge-based manipulation of genetic material. From a moral-philosophical perspective, this radical reification of the person is an absurdity: it contradicts elementary notions of human dignity. At the same time, the female subject becomes an object of population policy and biopolitics. In a liberal sense of justice, the follow-up question arises: shouldn't all women be given the opportunity to have their bodies medically modified until a certain optimum is achieved? The sheer mania for feasibility forces individuals in the direction of hyper-individualistic self-design, whereby in the context of the genetically controlled design of babies it is possibly a continuation of self-design on the externalised corpus vivendi with the means of reproductive technology. While it was once the clergymen who theologically appropriated women's wombs, today it is the more delicate material interventions in the germ line and the bodily system of women by medical men that manipulate fertilisation.

3 Practices of Design, Care, and Resistance as Utopian Powers

3.1 Care work and Neediness in the Anthropocene

In 2024, the Berlin Museum of Decorative Arts presented a programme with the promising title 'More than Human. Design after the Anthropocene' which implicitly echoes ecofeminist claims and raises design-philosophical questions such as:
 'Against the backdrop of the current climate crisis and growing scarcity of resources, disciplines such as architecture and design are also under scrutiny. The question therefore arises: What does 'more than human' mean for a design concept or for a design philosophy that focuses on people and their needs? What does design mean beyond the still valid modernist vision of progress? What alternative spaces for action open up beyond a production practice geared towards the exploitation of life forms and resources?' (https://www.museumsportal-berlin.de/de/ausstellungen/more-than-human/) (author's translation).
 This passage demonstrates in a paradigmatic way the dilemma designers face: on the one hand, they want to cope with the fact of achieve resource justice, while on the other hand, they still want to place people at the center. However, this is a conflict of values and objectives that cannot simply be resolved with design. Rather, there is a danger of causing additional damage to both human and non-human nature in the Anthropocene by focusing on human needs in an undifferentiated and uncritical manner. This is because it is easy to generalise certain established practices, which, from an ecofeminist perspective, should be put to the normative and axiological test: 'Values' are in turn not detached 'from practices' (Göpel/Redecker 2022: 32, author's translation), says feminist philosopher Eva von Redecker (*1982). Like many ecofeminist-inspired positions, she also prefers to operate in the spectrum between 'freedom and liberation: freedom from domination, freedom as free time, the freedom to have an open future', whereby 'in liberal modernity' these freedoms should be considered on the basis of rights, or more precisely, 'subjective individual rights, in relation to which equality now actually prevails' (ibid.: 60, author's translation). It should be noted

here that life, health and a certain subsistence level must logically precede freedom. And even then, the rights to freedom that apply equally to all have purely formal validity. But only de facto for those who can actually claim these rights as citizens. This only applies to a very limited extent to migrants, climate refugees or asylum seekers, for example. Part of the design of statehood is that we are citizens of a certain territory, which gives us a privileged or marginalised position in the legal system, depending on our nationality. This affiliation is in turn linked to specific life opportunities as prerequisites for freedom as well as the validity and observance of fundamental rights. The question of whether or not people or groups of people have equal opportunities or participatory justice is documented, as it were, on maps that depict the political order of things. What does not appear on these maps are concrete working and living conditions, which can be organized in a more egalitarian or less equitable way. What is not being noticed in the patriarchal setting is the economic contribution that women make through care work. Care work is an economy that is performed in the shadow of the 'post-industrial' family, in which the classic 'gender order' (Fraser 1994: 351, author's translation) has long since ceased to apply. Developing a design of care work that is fair for all those involved would be a commendable and intersectional task, in which the question 'HOW DO WE CARE' (Janssen / Tautfest 2021) could be at the center of experimental design processes. All genders should participate in these processes – also in the sense of a 'degendering' of care work, as Sherilyn MacGregor calls for:

> 'It is important to make a distinction between them, to say that people can care without being mothers and that caring can be generalised in a way that mothering cannot. But it is also necessary to acknowledge that although it is important to argue for a de-gendering of care, doing so will not change the association of the two in the popular discourse, and as such there will always be risks for feminists in adopting the discourse of care. So, I think both insights ought to be incorporated into an ecofeminist approach to citizenship. Concretely, to politicize care is to show its value as both an ethic and a practice in addressing issues of social and environmental justice and to note the similarities between the exploitation of women's caring work and 'natural' 'processes in the capitalist economy' (MacGregor 2004: 78f.).

Capitalism permanently benefits from the fact that women have to work as resources of reproductive labour without receiving a wage or a comparable equivalent; they perform 'work worth eleven trillion US dollars' (Hansen/Gerner 2024: 22, author's translation) every year without being paid. However, social welfare depends to a large extent on their practices as responsible citizens. Education, care and the resulting responsibilities are invaluable for the stability of a free and democratic society. Whether a price should be attached to these services, like other services, depends in the market economy on whether they are seen as productive activities or merely private practices. In this context, design could be given the task of transforming practices that are considered private into a social institution, as it were, which brings the standard of justice to bear and thereby links individual and situation-ethically relevant needs with social and public concerns in a meaningful and problem-sensitive way. The situational-ethical perspective is so important in this area because we are not dealing with equal relationships in care work, but rather with asymmetrical relationships nolens volens:

> 'We are used to raising autonomy and mutual recognition as equals to an ethical standard. It can be assumed that children are not yet fully able to protect and articulate their own interests. For this reason, others have a special responsibility for them, which is referred to as a duty of care. The 'duty of care for infants' as an ethical subject is so instructive for designers because there are 'moral situations' that are characterised by asymmetry: the relationship to children, the disabled, the infirm elderly, coma patients, etc. The constitution of restricted persons requires a special degree of empathy and a sense of responsibility on the part of the designers' (Bauer 2022: 45f., author's translation).

As can only be hinted at here, the morally valuable practices of care work, care and education require the study of human nature. This study is so instructive because it points us to ethical situations in which a particular neediness is present. Neediness is a basic anthropological category. It can teach us essential things about what life is in toto: vulnerability, mortality and finiteness, which are as elementary as they are vital to survival. The Spanish ecofeminist Yayo Herrero (*1965) has taken up this anthropological dimension. She uses the term 'ecodependence' to express how the awareness of our natural limits and our material constitution is related to the vulnerability of the system as a whole: 'Somos seres ecodependientes.' (Herrero 2016: 146) as an insight means for her that in 'capitalismo heteropatriarcal / heteropatriarchal capitalism' the sense of natural-material boundaries has been lost (ibid.).

In this confusion, on which heteropatriarchal capitalism is based, the usual organisational patterns for living together are also losing their grip. The distinction between private and public, which feminists fought against under the motto 'The private is public', collapses under the pressure of a no longer granted 'protection of society from the economy', which until recently could be 'equated with the defence of gender hierarchy' (Fraser 2023: 112, author's translation). The fact that the dualistic coding "private=female" responsible for social reproduction // "public=male" responsible for production is no longer particularly meaningful, is also demonstrated by developments in design. It is interesting to see that in contemporary speculative design, a third position is emerging in an experimental way, filled by (largely) gender-neutral robots that are supposed to be able, for example, to support parents in raising their children. However, the question arises: 'Would they like a robot to look after them?' (Kries et al. 2017: 202, author's translation).

However, this design gadget exemplifies a fundamental problem of 'liberal feminists', namely 'valuing the male-coded pursuit of autonomy more highly than the ideals of nurture and care that are seen as feminine' (Fraser 2023: 111, author's translation).

In late capitalism, the relationship between economy and politics has become deeply disturbed and the economic has become the omnipresent basic category; only that this has not led to the expansion of the feminine, which in any case meant an essentialisation from which the majority of today's ecofeminists distance themselves. Some representatives from the Global South with a postcolonial theoretical approach, on the other hand, opt for 'essentialisation' (à la Gayatri Spivak) for strategic reasons, i.e. they see 'a strategic political identification of women and nature' as an opportunity to create 'political[.] identities' (Hansen / Gerner 2024: 49, author's translation). Since the 1970s, this strategic framing has at least allowed resistance groups to characterise inhumane economic policies as hostile to women and life. This can only be countered with the sanctions of the law and the means of ethics. This thesis leads us to the final basic question: Why should designers concern themselves with ecofeminism?

3.2 Why Ecofeminism in Design? The Utopia of Natural Rights, Queer Ecologies and Inclusion

It makes sense for designers to engage with ecofeminism in order to visualise the material conditions under which the three major economies take place: 1) the economy of life, 2) the economy of subsistence and 3) the market economy. We are used to recognise the third economy, the market economy, as the universally valid principle and the standard economy. However, within the framework of an ecofeminist-inspired philosophy, it is conceivable and tangible to increasingly adjust socially and globally to the economy of subsistence and a corresponding 'subsistence perspective' (Mies/Bennholdt-Thomsen 2000). In her project 'Wandelmut: Eine Onlineplattform zur Promotion von Postwachstumsprojekten' (Königl 2018: 41–78), Kathrin Königl has exemplified how information and communication designers can contribute to shaping digital and political realities that are committed to the economy of subsistence within the framework of applied design research. This includes positions from the degrowth movement, the commons movement and other alternative, scientifically operating activists whose basic attitude is sceptical of capitalism.

These groups of people are keen to contain the massive interventions in human and non-human nature and reduce them to a tolerable, perhaps even healthy level. However, this healthy level can only be reached if we distance ourselves from a grand narrative of modernity – unlimited growth. This is opposed by the idea of natural rights. A 'right for Mother Nature', as provided for in some Latin American constitutions, is being discussed in one place or another in the EU. It is about nothing less than the recognition that the interconnectedness of all living beings is worthy of protection and about fundamental rights for the more-than-humans. Accordingly, for some years now, sustainability and environmental law have been advocating that nature should also be granted fundamental rights under constitutional law. In Germany, for example, the constitutional law expert Jens Kersten advocates such a position (Kersten 2020: 27–32). The idea of granting nature the status of a person and also a legal entity is of indigenous origin. Ecofeminists such as Vandana Shiva have popularised this idea. Contributions from the 'deep ecology' such as Arne Naess or holistically arguing ecofeminists such as Val Plumwood, Carolyn Merchant, Karen J. Warren and Maria Mies have also been used to formulate criticism of 'a false dualistic ontology', which contrasts 'Cartesian, Christian, male, Western thinking' and action with a holistic concept of nature (1997: 361f., author's translation). In internal academic discourse, the holism argument is generally given short shrift. However, it is recognised in one respect: the survival of the species is linked to nature conservation. But representatives of holism go much further.

They demand that "mother earth" should be included as a legal entity within the scope of fundamental rights. This legal-philosophical as well as natural and environmental ethical approach should be just as open to the next generation of designers as the nature-ethical design argument, according to which the aesthetic fascination that wild nature exerts on us humans also serves to relieve us: not only does nature have no opinion of us, it is also undistorted by man-made artefacts for which we bear 'responsibility for form' (ibid.: 374, author's translation). These sources of observation should be kept open in particular for designers who wish to familiarise themselves with the 'history of sustainable design' (Fuhs/Brocchi/Maxein 2013) and participate in a cultural evolution that takes the idea of resource justice seriously. At the same time, criticism of ecofeminist and deep ecology approaches can be expected from various directions: Firstly, the animist concepts and cosmological ideas of order do not appear to be compatible with the European value system – something that the representatives of ecofeminism largely admit themselves. Secondly, those interest groups or social institutions that stand up for the rights of Mother Earth are likely to come into conflict with liberal ideas of justice, such as those advocated by Rawls in 'Justice as Fairness'. Or, in the words of Sherilyn MacGregor: 'Please let us not forget that it [ecofeminist praxis] has never been liberal! It had always been materialist and anti-capitalist.' (Hansen/Gerner 2024: 17, author's translation). In the West, free and equal individuals are always assumed to be the bearers of property rights that occur in bourgeois world society.

Ideas of rights as actualised in an 'Earth democracy' (Shiva 2006), in which all living beings would potentially become bearers of rights and the parliament would become the place of democratic debate on the planetary common good, seem less compatible with this. But even in Western scientific theory, new alliances are emerging: This is supported by the philosophical speculation of thinkers such as Bruno Latour (1947–2022) and Michel Serres (1930–2019) to expand the site of the legislature to include an unimaginable number of organisms – an idea that Serres explored in his contractualist model of the 'natural contract' (The Natural Contract, 1994). Related approaches have found their way into scientific concepts, such as Latour's 'The Terrestrial Manifesto' (Latour 2018): Although Latour is not an explicit ecofeminist, he is nonetheless a legitimate heir to certain elements of the 'Gaia theory', which he adopted by means of the scientific theoretical positions of biologist Lynn Margulis (1938–2011) and atmospheric chemist James Lovelock (1919–2022). Both scientists are prominent representatives of the 'Gaia theory', which in turn has connections to deep ecology. Latour's range of theories has references to ecofeminist approaches where it concerns the soil (the terroir) as the ancestral home of people who count themselves among the colonised in both the material and immaterial sense and who sometimes fall into existential panic when this soil is torn from them:

> 'But where does the panic come from? From that deep-seated sense of injustice that has afflicted those who saw themselves deprived of their land during the conquests, then colonization, and finally during the era of 'development': a power from elsewhere is taking your territory and you can do nothing about it' (Latour 2018: 17, author's translation).

In design, these approaches are probably only familiar to a few because design is an integral part of a differentiating service society in which the 'creative class' (Richard Florida) is barely aware of the concerns and needs of agrarian societies. They neither take any notice of it, nor do they show much interest in the force and intensity of the interventions that the mining, food and energy industries are making worldwide in order to make resources available for industrial goods, which industrial, food or fashion designers may then also help to shape. Designers are usually uninformed about the extent of the exploitation of female workers in countries of the Global South. Although they are deeply involved in the globalization of economic cycles, they hardly feel emotionally or morally involved. A strong pinch of ecofeminism and an awareness of global production networks would do them no harm. As ecofeminist-inspired activists, communication designers could play an increasingly critical role in areas where supranational corporations are taking over territories that are vital for survival (land grabbing) and people are being deprived of their livelihoods due to changes in legal and climatic conditions. Some of these people are on the move and we then encounter them again in a hotly contested political arena: the migration debate. A debate in which ecofeminists find it difficult to assert themselves, as it is characterized by the utmost (petro)masculine aggression. Rational actors may take into account that Western nations are dependent on immigration in many respects due to their demographic development. However, there is no consensus on how to deal with climate refugees on a national level, for example. To a large extent, they are the victims of the lack of foresight on the part of actors in the Global North. The decisive factor for the acceptance of migrant actors will be whether it is possible to make their contribution to the common good visible in public discourse. Because then it is more likely that a balanced liberal conception of justice, as developed by Rawls, will also be accepted on the battlefield of political opinions.

Rawls conceptualised justice as a complex consisting of three basic principles: 'freedom, equality and reward for services that contribute to the common good' (Rawls 2020: 13). Ecofeminists as agents of social balance will rightly be able to point out that there is a major contribution to the common good that is made in the form of care work. With regard to the (form of) just and justifiable rewards (aka: remuneration) and the due appreciation of achievements, a feminist solidarity could emerge between domestic and foreign women that counters petromasculine overkill. In order for this solidarity to take political shape, new social institutions would have to be created that enable an 'egalitarian perspective' (Merchant 2020: xxix). After all, it remains questionable whether the traditional family is the appropriate social institution in which the 'normative claim of all people to be treated equally' (Mahadevan/Schmidt 2023: 635, author's translation) can be realised. Inequalities that arise on the basis of gender are quickly interpreted as natural. And this is an ideological trap into which ecofeminists can also fall, as Merchant already noted in her preface (Preface, 1990). There is a danger of 'essentialism' precisely where women bring themselves too close to nature in the context of reproductive biology (ibid.: xxiv). And the other danger of our time is hyper-individualism, i.e. the denial of the ecological and social foundations of our existence – the connection with all living things. Ecofeminism is constantly evolving and, under the banner of 'queer ecologies', is expanding its perspectives 'to include a critique of heteronormativity' (Bauhardt 2019, 467, author's translation). In all its varieties, it is a kind of intellectual and activist resistance movement that is repeatedly coming to light in various places around the world because women and, more recently, queer people are resisting: they are protesting against heteropatriarchal capitalism, which often enough has the character of a crime against humanity and against the dignity of Mother Earth. People in the Chipko movement in India, the Green Belt movement in Kenya or the 'Love Canal movement' in the USA (Hansen/Gerner 2024: 54 f.) could no longer bear to see their material livelihoods destroyed. These protest movements emerged as a reaction to blatant environmental destruction and the destruction of life opportunities, especially for women and children as well as future generations. Basically, they also represent seedlings that continue to have an effect in 'Fridays for future', 'Extinction Rebellion', 'Last Generation' and 'Ende Gelände' in that these protest movements are also about addressing or claiming the rights of future generations. In some cases, certain actors or groups of actors from these movements come into conflict with existing state law, although they have repeatedly succeeded in asserting themselves in the public eye as representatives of the just cause.

Their counterpart is the petromasculine elite worldwide, which is causing a shift towards authoritarianism even in liberal democracies. The ecofeminist point of view, on the other hand, is a radically democratic one, namely one that also sees the issue of biodiversity, for example, as a question of democracy, namely natural diversity. In the background are concepts of democracy and legal concepts that originate from non-European traditions. And last but not least, the point of view is a radically inclusive one, a point that is likely to bring ecofeminists into conversation with current design movements (Mareis/Paim 2021). Discussing the analyses of ecofeminists and trying out their theses could prove to be a concrete utopia in which the hope for 'a new world order that entails changing contemporary conceptions of what nature is, what it means to be human, and what it means to be ethical' (Glazebrook 2002: 24) can come together in a meaningful way.

References

Bauer, C. (2021): Schädliches Design. Demoralisierende Designtheorie?. In: Rodatz, C./Smolarski, P. (eds.) Wie können wir den Schaden maximieren? Gestaltung trotz Komplexität. Beiträge zu einem Public Interest Design. Bielefeld: Transcript, 59–78.

Bauer, C. (2022): Ethik für Designer. Stuttgart: av Edition.

Bauer, C. (2024): Der Wille zur Nachhaltigkeit. In: Bund Deutscher Architektinnen und Architekten BDA (ed.): Die Architektin, Nr. 4, 2024. Berlin: Res Publica Verlag.

Bauhardt, C. (2019): Ökofeminismus und Queer Ecologies: feministische Analyse gesellschaftlicher Naturverhältnisse. In: Kortendiek, B./Riegraf, B./Sabisch, K. (eds.): Handbuch Interdisziplinäre Geschlechterforschung (=Geschlecht und Gesellschaft, Vol. 65). Wiesbaden: Springer VS, 467–477. https://doi.org/10.1007/978-3-658-12496-0_159

Carson, R. (2000) [1962]: The Silent Spring. Dublin: Penguin Modern Classics.

Constanza-Chock, S. (2020): Design Justice. Community-led practices to build the worlds we need. Cambridge/London: MIT Press.

D'Eaubonne, F. (2022) [1974]: Feminism or Death. How the Women's Movement Can Save the Planet. London: Verso Books.

Daggett, Cara New (2024): Petromaskulinität. Fossile Energieträger und autoritäres Begehren. Berlin: Mattes & Seitz.

Ekardt, F./Winter, A. (2023): Umweltethik. In: Frühbauer, J. et al: Rawls- Handbuch. Leben – Werk – Wirkung. Berlin: J.B. Metzler, 623–632. http://doi.org/10.1007/978-3-476- 05928-4_79

Förster, A. (2023): Gerechtigkeit als Fairneß. In: Frühbauer, J. et al.: Rawls-Handbuch. Leben – Werk – Wirkung. Berlin: J.B. Metzler, 63–73. http://doi.org/10.1007/978-3-476- 05928-4_6

Fuhs, K.-S./ Brocchi, D./Maxein, M. (2013): Die Geschichte des Nachhaltigen Designs. Welche Haltung braucht Gestaltung. Bad Homburg: VAS.

Fraser, N. (1994): Die Gleichheit der Geschlechter und das Wohlfahrtssystem. Ein postindustrielles Gedankenexperiment. In: Honneth, A. (ed.): Pathologien des Sozialen. Die Aufgaben der Sozialphilosophie. Frankfurt am Main: Fischer Verlag, 351–376.

Fraser, N. (2023): Der Allesfresser. Wie der Kapitalismus seine eigenen Grundlagen verschlingt, Berlin: Suhrkamp Verlag.

Göpel, M./v. Redecker, E. (2022): Schöpfen und Erschöpfen. Ed. by Maximilian Haas u. Margarita Tsomou. Berlin: Matthes & Seitz.

Glazebrook, T.: Karen Warren's Ecofeminism. In: Ethics and the Environment, Autumn, 2002, Vol. 7, No. 2 (Autumn, 2002). Indiana University Press, 12–26; URL: https://www.jstor.org/stable/40339034

Hansen, L./ Gerner, N. (2024): Ökofeminismus. Zwischen Theorie und Praxis. Eine Einführung. Münster: Unrast-Verlag.

Herrero, Y. (2016): Feminist economics and Urgent Dialogue. In: Revista de Economía Crítica, n°22, segundo semester, 144–161. Internet-Source: https://base.socioeco.org/docs/yayoherrero_economia-feminista.pdf

Janssen, J./Tautfest, A. (eds.) (2021): KANON – Die experimentelle Klasse. Hamburg: Argument Verlag mit Ariadne.

Kaiser, A./Stephany, R. (eds.) (2021): Glossary of undisciplined Design. Leipzig: Spector Books.

Kersten, J. (2020): Natur als Rechtssubjekt. Für eine ökologische Revolution des Rechts. In: Bundeszentrale für politische Bildung (ed.): Aus Politik und Zeitgeschichte. 70. Jahrgang, 11/2020, 27–32.

Königl, K. (2018): Wandelmut: Eine Onlineplattform zur Promotion von Postwachstumsprojekten. In: Bauer, C./Niederauer, M./Schweppenhäuser, G.: Gestaltung digitaler und politischer Wirklichkeiten (=Würzburger Beiträge zur Designforschung, Bd. 1). Wiesbaden: Springer Verlag, 41–78.

Krebs, A. (1997): Naturethik im Überblick. In: Krebs, Angelika (ed.): Naturethik. Grundtexte der gegenwärtigen tier- und ökoethischen Diskussion. Frankfurt am Main: Suhrkamp Verlag, 337–379.

Kries, M./Thun-Hohenstein, C./Klein, A. (eds.) (2017): Hello, Robot. Design zwischen Mensch und Maschine. Ausstell.-Kat.Vitra Design Museum/MAK/Design Museum Gent.

MacGregor, S. (2004): From Care to Citizenship. Calling Ecofeminism back to Politics. In: Ethics & Environment, 9(1) 2004. Indiana University Press, 57–84.

Mahadevan, K./Schmidt, T. (2023): Feminismus und Care-Arbeit. In: Frühbauer, J. et al.: Rawls-Handbuch. Leben – Werk – Wirkung. Berlin: J.B. Metzler, 635–643. http://doi.org/10.1007/978- 3-476-05928-4_80

Mareis, C./Paim, N. (eds.) (2021): Design Struggles. Intersecting Histories, Pedagogies, and Perspectives, Amsterdam: Valiz.

Marx, K. (2009): Ökonomisch-philosophische Manuskripte. Comment by Michael Quante. Frankfurt am Main: Suhrkamp Verlag.

Merchant, C. (2020): The Death of Nature. Women, Ecology, and the Scientific Revolution. Harper Collins Publishers: New York: Fortieth Anniversary Edition.

Mies, M./Bennholdt-Thomsen, V. (2000): The Subsistence Perspective: Beyond the Globalized Economy. London: Zed Books.

Mies, Maria (2015): Patriarchat & Kapital. Munich: bge-Verlag.

Mies, M./Shiva, V. (2016): Ökofeminismus. Die Befreiung der Frauen, der Natur und unterdrückter Völker. Eine neue Welt wird geboren. Neu-Ulm: AG SPAK Bücher.

Latour, B. (2018): Das terristrische Manifest. Berlin: Suhrkamp Verlag.

Rawls, J. (1975): Eine Theorie der Gerechtigkeit. Frankfurt am Main: Suhrkamp Verlag.

Rawls, J. (2020): Justice as Fairness. Gerechtigkeit als Fairness. English/German. Ditzingen: Reclam.

Salleh, A. (2017): Ecofeminism as Politics. Nature, Marx, and the Postmodern. London: Zed Books.

Shiva, V. (2006): Erd-Demokratie: Alternativen zur neoliberalen Globalisierung. Zürich: Rotpunkt-Verlag.

Serres, M. (1994): Der Naturvertrag. Frankfurt am Main: Suhrkamp Verlag.

Warren, K. J. (2020): Ecofeminist Philosophy: A Western Perspective on What It Is and Why It Matters. New York: Rowman and Littlefield.

von Werlhof, C./Mies, M./Bennholdt-Thomsen, V. (1988): Frauen, die letzte Kolonie. Zur Hausfrauisierung der Arbeit. Reinbek: Rowohlt Verlag.

An Intersectional Design Approach to Sustainable and Inclusive Futures

Hannah Jones and Londa Schiebinger

This chapter reflects upon creating design tools for intersectional innovation, a new approach to tackling social and environmental inequities, largely in the realm of emerging technologies. The chapter presents the Intersectional Design Cards – a collaborative tool developed to support teams in creating radically inclusive products, processes and paradigms. The chapter makes use of the cards to map and explore intersectional factors, design questions and case studies related to four design levels. These levels include the form and function of a design, the experiences and services that a design might offer, the systems and infrastructures that a design connects to and the new paradigms and purpose that a design might catalyse. The chapter discusses where design has failed in terms of fairness and where design can find new opportunities for achieving greater sustainability for our societies and our planet. Further examples focus on how the cards have been used with students and professionals in the design industry, including from our 'Innovations in Inclusive Design' class at the Hasso Plattner Institute of Design (d.school), Stanford University, US, to inform the creation of intersectional design concepts.

Introduction

Today, the advent of new AI technologies brings with them a host of new issues. For example, in a recent study of racial disparities in automated speech recognition systems, five leading providers (including Amazon, Apple, Google, IBM and Microsoft) were audited to compare human and machine generated transcripts for Black and White speakers. The study found that the AI error rates were twice as great for Black as for White speakers. And when gender was factored in, the technology performed particularly poorly for Black men. The issue here is insufficient audio data from Black speakers. Varied demographic data collection, including African American Vernacular English and other varieties of English, is needed to create products that work globally (Koenecke et al.: 2020). How might design teams avoid discriminating against marginalised communities and better understand the consequences of their designs, to create more equitable solutions from the outset?

Here we present the Intersectional Design Cards – a collaborative tool developed to support teams in creating radically inclusive products, processes and paradigms. Our tool was developed over seven years in a class entitled 'Innovations in Inclusive Design' (previously called 'Beyond Pink and Blue: Gender in Tech') at Stanford's d.school. Our design tool integrated research concepts and methods from Gendered Innovations (http://genderedinnovations.stanford.edu), a research platform that harnesses the 'creative power of sex, gender and intersectional analysis for innovation and discovery' into the design process. Our goal in this work is to introduce the world of design to a systemic design process aimed at producing socially and environmentally inclusive and transformative outcomes.

This chapter makes use of our design cards to demonstrate the potential of applying intersectional thinking to design practice. We use a selection of our case studies to propose how design can be transformed by intersectional approaches that address multiple forms of discrimination and ultimately better serve the needs of diverse users.

Why do we need Intersectional Design?

Figure 1: Moving from a single-axis analysis to embracing multiple factors for innovation.

Jones, Schiebinger, Grimes and Small, 2021

In 1989, legal scholar Kimberlé Crenshaw coined the term intersectionality to describe how multiple forms of discrimination, power and privilege intersect in Black women's lives, in ways that are erased when sexism and racism are treated separately (Crenshaw: 1989). Since then, the term has been expanded to describe intersecting forms of oppression and inequality emerging from structural advantages and disadvantages that shape a person's or a group's experience and social opportunities (Collins & Bilge: 2020). In short, 'intersectionality' considers how one person can face several different forms of discrimination at the same time. A person is not simply a woman, for example, but also has a particular ethnicity and class background, and may also be a single head of household or from the Global South.

If we apply this thinking to design, intersectionality, then, moves beyond a traditional notion of 'inclusive design' (Clarkson & Coleman: 2015) that takes as its starting point a single axis of discrimination, such as age or disability to the expansive idea of 'intersectional design' that identifies multiple, intersecting factors, such as age, disability, and gender (fig. 1). This paradigm shift is also championed in Sasha Costanza-Chock's notion of 'design justice' (Costanza-Chock: 2018). Intersectional design seeks to enhance socially equity and environmental sustainability while at the same time uncovering new design opportunities (Buolamwini & Gebru: 2018).

Our work as designers, educators and researchers has been to introduce intersectional analysis to interdisciplinary design teams to facilitate inclusive approaches that generate new products, services and systems. Our challenge has been to integrate these concepts and methods into different stages of the design process in efforts to enrich vocabulary, address biases and assumptions, and generate innovative concepts and prototypes that broaden the frame of inclusivity. Here we describe our tool for intersectionality – our Intersectional Design Cards – which received a Notable Distinction for the Core 77 Design Education Initiative Award, 2022.

How can a Design Team get the Conversation Started?

Our design cards are composed of three sets, including:
- SET 1: 12 Intersectional Definition cards
- SET 2: 12 Design Question cards
- SET 3: 16 Case Study cards with intersectional factors

These sets are accompanied by a guide booklet that includes an introduction to the cards and some starter activities.

A key purpose of the first set of intersectional definition cards is to dynamically evolve the vocabulary used in design to include definitions relevant to different cultures and different professional disciplines. We recognise that these definitions might mean something different to different people and might be uncomfortable to discuss. This definitional part of the design process may not result in complete agreement, but hopefully it expands a team's cultural awareness and helps to develop a shared language early in the process.

Importantly, the intersectional factors teams choose will depend on the culture(s) they are designing for. The cards may help co-design teams tune into the needs of a local context, or alternatively, assist large companies in global markets; e.g. Tesla or Toyota, for example, do not sell cars only in the US or Japan, but throughout the world.

The 16 design case studies included in our cards include – but are not limited to – the following 12 factors:

Table 1: 12 Intersectional Factors addressed in the design cards' case studies.

Age	Geographic Location
Disability	Race
Educational Background	Sex
Ethnicity	Sexuality
Family Configuration	Social and Economic Status (SES)
Gender	Sustainability

In our deck, we also offer blank factors cards for teams to fill in factors pertinent to their projects. During our classes and workshops, participants have highlighted factors, such as housing status, Indigeneity, mental health, migration status, neurodiversity, non-human animals, pollution, spiritual traditions, and more.

Apple product designers have also recently proposed the 18 diversity axes that they emphasise aim to 'empower and delight everyone' (Apple WWDC: 2021).

Table 2: Apple's 18 Diversity Axes.

Abilities	Handedness
Age	Language
Class	Location
Connectivity	Modern Technology
Disabilities	Philosophical Beliefs
Education	Political Beliefs
Environmental Conditions	Race
Ethnicity	Religion
Gender	Sexual Orientation

'Handedness' is interesting here. We know, for example, a world-class surgeon who is left-handed. When she trained, and still largely today, surgical instruments are designed for right-handed people. Think how even more advanced her techniques might be if the instruments had suited her needs rather than her needing to adapt to them. 'Handedness' may also be important in human-robot interaction during a 'handover task.'

Intersectional factors are culturally specific. Both sets of factors highlighted here (table 1 and 2) were developed in the US. Europeans tell us, for example, they cannot include 'race' because many European governments forbid, since World War II, collecting such data. But because much design is global, teams may still need to consider it. An important factor missing here is caste, which operates in important way in South Asia and, as new studies have revealed, in Silicon Valley (Paul: 2021).

A second point to make here is that each design team needs to choose the factors most relevant to their product or service. A team cannot look at all the factors. As in any research project, designers start with a wide purview that they subsequently narrow. The important point is that their choice of factors should result from a defined process – and should not rely on unconscious defaults.

An Expanded Definition of Design

In our classes, we pose the question: 'How might we create a toolkit for design and engineering teams that is responsive to intersectional needs and perspectives?' To facilitate the process, we developed an expanded definition of design, organised into four design levels that scale-up from the physical characteristics of a design (form & function) to the more intangible, cultural aspects (paradigms & purposes) (fig. 2). We illustrate these four levels through the example of a smartphone.

Figure 2: Four Levels of Design. Intersectional Design Cards.

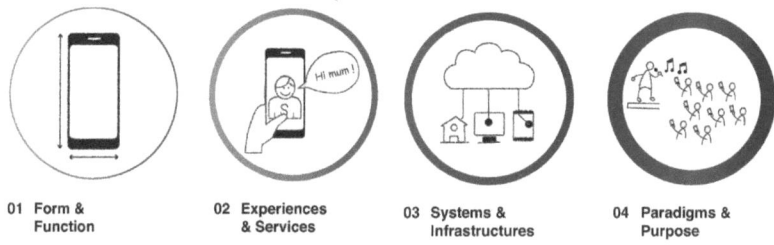

01 Form &
    Function

02 Experiences
    & Services

03 Systems &
    Infrastructures

04 Paradigms &
    Purpose

Guide to the Intersectional Design Cards. (Jones, Schiebinger, Grimes and Small, 2021, p. 12–13)

Design might focus on form and function, i.e. the look and feel of the device in your hand. It might seek to enhance experiences and services, i.e. the pleasure of video chatting or the distress of a poorly functioning virtual assistant. It might extend to systems and infrastructures that network hardware and software to larger systems, i.e. tackling privacy and data protection issues using cloud-based software. Or it might capture new paradigms and purposes, i.e. support cultural trends that emerge through using the device in new and unforeseen ways. For example, an industrial designer might consider the look and feel of a product, while a computer scientist might work to perfect automated speech recognition systems. A sustainable design researcher might consider the life-cycle assessment of a product, or a futures-orientated team might look at how emerging technologies can encourage new behaviours or social interaction. This expansive definition of design enables teams to evaluate equity and inclusion across a broad spectrum, pinpointing where their work can have the greatest impact.

How the Cards Work Together in Our Four Design Levels

In this section, we select and arrange cards from our deck to illustrate how the intersectional factors cards figure in design questions at each design level through specific case studies.

1. Designing for Form & Function

Case studies: Pulse Oximeters & Inclusive Crash Test Dummies
Design question: Who is the user?
Intersectional factors: Age, Ethnicity, Gender, Race, Sex

Figure 3: Designing for Form & Function. Intersectional Design Cards.

Jones, Schiebinger, Grimes and Small, 2021

Pulse Oximeters

As we learned during the COVID-19 pandemic, pulse oximeters may not work well for people with darker skin. Patented in 1972, pulse oximeters are able to measure oxygen levels without drawing arterial blood and are among the first defenders in emergency rooms. Yet, pulse oximeters may overestimate arterial oxyhaemoglobin saturation in patients with darker pigmented skin. Why is that? Interestingly, both deoxyhaemoglobin in the blood and melanin in skin absorb light, meaning that the accuracy of devices that use infrared and red light signaling may vary with skin tone. A recent study that analysed some 47,000 patients found that oximeters misread blood gases 12 percent of the time in Black patients compared to 4 percent of the time in White patients. Patients who do not receive supplemental oxygen when needed are put at risk for organ failure (Sjoding et al.: 2020).

Oximeters can also be inaccurate for women, whose fingers are typically smaller and geometrically different from men's. From an intersectional perspective, Black women may experience the highest error rates. How might oximeters be redesigned to meet the needs of all users?

Crash Test Dummies

Female drivers are 47% more likely to sustain severe injuries than males in comparable crashes, when controlling for body mass. Crash test dummies have been designed to represent the mid-sized male (1.75 m/78 kg); the 5th percentile female dummy (1.50 m/49 kg) is simply a scaled-down version of this male norm. These small dummies are often placed in the passenger's seat, which reinforces gender stereotypes and fails to protect women drivers.

Older people are more likely to experience serious injuries in almost every crash type, and older women are at greatest risk for bone fracture.

Asian populations are on average smaller by height and weight than US adults. In an intersectional innovation, Matt Reed at the University of Michigan has developed virtual dummies that adjust by height, weight, and age for both US and Japanese populations (Hu et al.: 2012).

2. Designing for Experiences & Services

Case study: Smart Mobility & Virtual Assistants
Design question: Who might be marginalized within your target demographic?
Intersectional factors: Age, Ethnicity, Gender, Sexuality

Figure 4: Designing for Experiences & Services. Intersectional Design Cards.

Jones, Schiebinger, Grimes and Small, 2021

Smart Mobility

Numerous innovations surround safety concerns for women, LGBTQ+ individuals, and older people. One such service is SafetiPin, developed in Delhi, India, in response to the fatal gang rape of a 23-year-old woman in 2012. Using a crowd-sourced mapping survey approach and safety audits, SafetiPin calculates the safest route between two locations. Using democratised mapping software encourages a broader range of users and helps break down societal barriers, including class and race. Also, importantly, it provides anonymity to users – allowing women and gender-diverse people, who wish to recount instances of gender-based violence but do not want to disclose their identity, to express their safety concerns (Martire et al.: 2023). Safety information can be shared with city authorities; Delhi, for example, improved lighting in over 5,000 locations in response to user data. SafetiPin now operates in 63 cities across 16 countries (Viswanath & Basu: 2015).

Virtual Assistants

Voice Assistants have primarily been gendered female, reinforcing negative stereotypes of female servitude. In 2019, a group of Danish researchers collaborated to develop "Q," the first genderless AI voice (Yalcinkaya: 2019). The database powering the voice was constructed by combining strands of gender-fluid humans' speech to reach a genderless range that is difficult for humans to categorise as either female or male. In this way, designers hope to add a viable gender-neutral option for voicing virtual assistants.

For conversational Voice Assistants to avoid bias, they must understand something about users' gender, age, ethnicity, geographic location, etc. Black English and particularly Black slang, for example, may be filtered out by algorithms designed to detect rudeness and hate speech.

2. Designing for Systems & Infrastructure

Case study: Menstrual Cups & Transportation Planning
Design question: How might your design change as social or environmental relations change in the coming years?
Intersectional factors: Family Configuration, Gender, Sex, Sustainability

Figure 5: Designing for Systems & Infrastructures. Intersectional Design Cards.

Jones, Schiebinger, Grimes and Small, 2021

Menstrual Cups

Environmental sustainability has become a top priority in this time of climate catastrophe (Raworth: 2017). Can intersectional analyses provide insights into solutions? Evidence suggests that changes in menstrual products can help achieve the United Nations' Sustainable Development Goals (SDG) #6 'clean water and sanitation' by the year 2030.2 A life-cycle assessment of six menstrual products (pads [organic and non-organic], tampons [organic and non-organic], menstrual cups and menstrual underwear across three countries (France, India, and the US) revealed that menstrual cups and menstrual underwear were the most sustainable, even in scenarios where these two products were used together (a common practice among menstruators) (Fourcassier et al.: 2022).

Menstrual cups may also contribute to the UN's SDG #5 'gender equality.' In cultures where women cannot say 'no' to sex, a menstrual cup can deliver contraception. It can also deliver vaginal medication, and, when a microbicide is added, adds protection against sexually transmitted infections and HIV. Where desired, it can also function as a fertility aid by retaining semen close to the cervix. More broadly, menstrual cups create a much-needed shift in the culture of menstruation and provide an example of a design solution that initiates a systemic change. Governments need to work with industry, educators and menstruators to drive environmental sustainability. Menstrual cups provide a great example of intersectional design, satisfying multiple needs and providing a glimpse into the kinds of alternative, sustainable future systems our products might materialise.

Transportation Planning

Do our cities support caregivers? Transportation planners collect data by journey purpose to plan infrastructure. Traditional data categories include, for example, employment, education and shopping. None of these categories capture carework – caring for children, the elderly and households – even though, when counted separately, "care-related trips," become the second largest category by trip purpose.

Why is this important? Caregivers tend to make 'chained' trips – or multiple, short trips that are grouped together rather than one long commute trip. Taking into consideration caregiver travel patterns allows transportation engineers to design systems that work efficiently across broader segments of the population. For example, how might future automated vehicles, their infrastructures, and services better address 'mobilities of care' (Sánchez de Madariaga/ Zucchini: 2019) to create more inclusive transportation systems?

3. Designing for Paradigms & Purpose

Case studies: Social Robots & Marine Science
Design question: What kinds of future worlds would you like to see your designs working in?
Intersectional factors: Disability, Gender, Race, Sex, Social and Economic Status, Sustainability

Figure 6: Designing for Paradigms & Purpose. Intersectional Design Cards.

Jones, Schiebinger, Grimes and Small, 2021

Social Robots

Should assistive social robots be gendered? If the robot is a nursing robot, should it be gendered female to match user expectations? We must remember that globally 90 % of nurses are women. If the robot meets user expectations, will the patient be more compliant? Will the patient be more likely to take the medicine or do the exercise the robot recommends?

It is important to remember that robots are designed in a world alive with gender norms, gender identities, and gender relations. Gender norms – in the workplace, in family culture, in institutional policies, etc. – are those spoken and unspoken cultural attitudes that influence our behaviours.3 Humans – whether as designers designing the robots or users using the robots – tend to gender machines (because, in human culture, gender remains a primary social category).

But there is a danger here. As soon as users gender a machine, stereotypes follow. The danger is that gendering robots may reinforce gender inequalities by embodying current stereotypes. Designing hardware, i.e., robots, toward current stereotypes may amplify those stereotypes into the future.

Gender issues can be compounded by intersecting issues related to skin tone. Social critics point out that most robots are white – plastic to be sure – but white nonetheless, and many have blue eyes, which may be problematic from a race/ethnicity point of view. Interestingly, we found one robot that can be customised for skin tone and gender. Carver is a darker skin toned robot designed for learners with autism spectrum disorder, and Milo is a lighter skin toned robot with the same function. Until recently, Robokind, the company behind the robots, offered only boy-like robots. But the company subsequently released Veda, a lighter-skin toned girl, and Jemi, a darker-skin toned girl. This is important because even though autism affects four times as many boys as girls, we need a teaching robot for the millions of girls suffering from the disorder. We cannot not tell if these robots are nonbinary or transgender.

From an intersectional point of view, the challenge to roboticists is to understand how social norms become embodied in robots – and, importantly, design robots to promote social equity.

Marine Science

Global warming is hurting marine organisms – a concern for all of us today. And, importantly, whether we are talking about fish, mollusks, crustaceans or other marine organisms, responses to global warming can vary by sex. And marine organisms are evolutionarily imaginative when it comes to sex. Did you know that in many marine organisms, such as turtles, sex is determined by temperature? Other sea creatures morph from one sex to another. Some are protandrous hermaphrodites – starting life as male, then changing into female. Others are protogynous hermaphrodites – starting as female, then changing into male. Analysing sex-based responses to climate change enables better modeling of demographic change among marine organisms and downstream impacts on humans.

Why is this important? For species reliant on temperature for sex determination, such as turtles, rapid global warming poses a risk to sex ratios and the stability of populations. The sex of a turtle, for example, depends on the temperature. If the climate is warmer, eggs hatch as females; if the climate is cooler, they hatch as males. An important study found that turtle sex ratios respond dramatically to global warming. In Australia, turtles born in warmer northern Great Barrier Reef, for instance, became 99% female, while cooler southern sites they remained a more natural 68% female. Such changes in sex balance can lead to population collapse. If a population is 99% female, it is hard for it to reproduce (Jensen et al.: 2018).

Sex changes may also be influenced by social status. Clownfish, for example, live in a strict social hierarchy with a single dominant female at the top, who matures and mates with a single large male. Removal of the alpha female results in the alpha male changing their sex to female, with all subordinates moving up a rung on the social ladder.

Analysing sex-based responses to climate change enables better modelling of demographic change among marine organisms and downstream impacts on humans. Effective ocean management and mitigation of climate change impacts depend on understanding organism and ecosystem responses to anthropogenic and environmental change (Gissi et al.: 2023).

How can we reframe our thinking to embrace our interspecies needs – moving beyond human-centred design to a new planetary genre of living systems-centred design? Our Lebenswelt is also that of the clown fish and sea turtle.

Insights from our Classes and Workshops

The illustrative examples above demonstrate how a team might engage with the cards to unpack intersectional issues and explore new pathways for innovation. In this section we briefly introduce two design examples from our classes and workshops that provide further insights into applying intersectional thinking to the design process.

1. Randi – A Concept for a Radically Inclusive Virtual Assistant

As part of the 'Beyond Pink and Blue: Gender in Tech' class Spring Quarter 2020, a group of Stanford students examined virtual assistants through an intersectional design lens. In response to their user research, one team posed the question 'How might we neutralise stereotypes perpetuated by virtual assistants?' They developed RANDI, a virtual assistant that randomly changed its identity. On any day, users could expect RANDI to generate new identity features, including race, ethnicity, gender, age, sexual orientation, pronouns and other general personality traits.4 This design idea is intended to maximise users' intercultural competence and empathy by increasing exposure to diverse identities, thus, challenging the industry's overuse of female stereotypes for virtual assistants (West et al.: 2019).

2. fAIr – A Pensions Gap Start-up Initiative

To celebrate the launch of the cards in April 2022 and to mark the opening of the Silicon Valley Archive at Stanford University, we were invited to exhibit the cards and run a workshop. For the workshop we invited start-up companies, associated with Nordic Innovation House in Silicon Valley, to use cards to enhance their inclusive innovations. Swedish innovators Lykke de Vries and Kamil Szczesny introduced their start-up fAIr, designed to address the 31% pension savings gap between men and women in Sweden.5 For them, the cards opened potentially 'unexplored problem areas, such as geographical location or social and economic status.' Working with the cards encouraged the team to think critically about how people would use fAIr's pension savings app and the features that they would need to include.

Summary

The examples we have presented in this chapter illustrate how intersectional design can transform a system, prototype solutions and help us imagine worlds that foster social equity and environmental sustainability. It is crucial for design to address equity – from the very beginning of the creative process. To do this, we have introduced our Intersectional Design Cards that help users better understand where design can find new opportunities for achieving greater sustainability for our societies and our planet. We offer illustrative case studies and ask design questions across four design levels in an effort to tell more comprehensive stories about how products and technologies shape lived experiences and to assist teams to engage in richer, more diverse, intersectional design thinking.

Acknowledgments

Thanks to the students from Beyond Pink and Blue: Gender in Tech and Innovations in Inclusive Design (2016-2022), and to our co-teachers Ann Grimes and Andrea Small.

References

Apple WWDC. (2021). The Process of Inclusive Design. https://developer.apple.com/videos/play/wwdc2021/10304/.

Buolamwini, J./ Gebru, T. (2018). Gender Shades: Intersectional Accuracy Disparities in Commercial Gender Classification. Proceedings of the 1st Conference on Fairness, Accountability and Transparency, 77–91. https://proceedings.mlr.press/v81/buolamwini18a.html

Collins, P. H./ Bilge, S. (2020). Intersectionality. New Jersey: John Wiley & Sons.

Costanza-Chock, S. (2021). Design Justice: Towards an Intersectional Feminist Framework for Design Theory and Practice. In C. Mareis & N. Paim (Eds.), Design Struggles: Intersecting Histories, Pedagogies, and Perspectives (pp. 333–353). Amsterdam: Valiz.

Crenshaw, K. (1989). Demarginalizing the Intersection of Race and Sex: A Black Feminist Critique of Antidiscrimination Doctrine, Feminist Theory and Antiracist Politics. University of Chicago Legal Forum, 1, 139-167. http://chicagounbound.uchicago.edu/uclf/vol1989/iss1/8

Fourcassier, S., Douziech, M., Pérez-López, P., & Schiebinger, L. (2022). Menstrual Products: A Comparable Life Cycle Assessment. Cleaner Environmental Systems, 7, 100096. https://doi.org/10.1016/j.cesys.2022.100096

Gissi, E./ Schiebinger, L./ Santoleri, R./ Micheli, F. (2023). Sex Analysis in Marine Biological Systems: Insights and Opportunities. Frontiers in Ecology and the Environment. June 13. https://doi.org/10.1002/fee.2652

Hu, J./Rupp, J. D./ Reed, M. P. (2012). Focusing on Vulnerable Populations in Crashes: Recent Advances in Finite Element Human Models for Injury Biomechanics Research. Journal of Automotive Safety and Energy, 3(4), 295–307.

Jensen, M. P./Allen, C. D., Eguchi, T., Bell, I. P., LaCasella, E. L., Hilton, W. A., … & Dutton, P. H. (2018). Environmental Warming and Feminization of One of the Largest Sea Turtle Populations in the World. Current Biology, 28(1), 154-159. https://doi.org/10.1016/j.cub.2017.11.057

John Clarkson, P./ Coleman, R. (2015). History of Inclusive Design in the UK. Applied Ergonomics, 46, 235–247. https://doi.org/10.1016/j.apergo.2013.03.002

Jones, H., Schiebinger, L., Grimes, A., and Small, A., (2021). Intersectional Design Cards: A Design Activity to Create Radically Inclusive Products, Processes, and Paradigms. Distributed by Stanford University Press. [online] Available at: www.intersectionaldesign.com [Accessed 19th June 2025].

Jones, H., Schiebinger, L., Grimes, A., and Small, A., (2021). Guide to the Intersectional Design Cards: A Design Activity to Create Radically Inclusive Products, Processes, and Paradigms. Distributed by Stanford University Press. [online] Available at: https://intersectionaldesign.com/download-guide-booklet/ [Accessed 19th June 2025].

Koenecke, A./ Nam, A./ Lake, E./ Nudell/ J., Quartey/ M., Mengesha/ Z., Toups/ C., Rickford/ J. R., Jurafsky/ D./ Goel, S. (2020). Racial Disparities in Automated Speech Recognition. Proceedings of the National Academy of Sciences, 117(14), 7684–7689. https://doi.org/10.1073/pnas.1915768117

Martire, A./ Hausleitner, B./ Clossick, J. (Eds.). (2023). Everyday Streets: Inclusive Approaches to Understanding and Designing Streets. Chicago: UCL Press. https://press.uchicago.edu/ucp/books/book/distributed/E/bo208645530.html

Paul, S. (n.d.). Trapped in Silicon Valley's Hidden Caste System. Wired. Retrieved July 31, 2023, from https://www.wired.com/story/trapped-in-silicon-valleys-hidden-caste-system/

Raworth, K. (2017). Doughnut Economics: Seven Ways to Think Like a 21st-Century Economist. Vermont: Chelsea Green Publishing.

Sánchez de Madariaga, I./ Zucchini, E. (2019). Measuring Mobilities of Care, a Challenge for Transport Agendas: From One to Many Tracks. In C. L. Scholten/ T. Joelsson (Eds.), Integrating Gender into Transport Planning: From One to Many Tracks (1st ed. 2019 edition, pp. 145–173). London: Palgrave Macmillan.

Sjoding, M. W./ Dickson, R. P./ Iwashyna, T. J./ Gay, S. E./ Valley, T. S. (2020). Racial Bias in Pulse Oximetry Measurement. New England Journal of Medicine, 383(25), 2477-2478. https://doi.org/10.1056/NEJMc2029240

Viswanath, K./ Basu, A. (2015). SafetiPin: An innovative Mobile App to Collect Data on Women's Safety in Indian Cities. Gender & Development, 23(1), 45–60. https://doi.org/10.1080/13552074.2015.1013669

West, M./ Kraut, R./ Chew, H. E. (2019). I'd Blush if I Could: Closing Gender Divides in Digital Skills through Education. UNESCO and EQUALS Skills Coalition.

Yalcinkaya, G. (2019). Q is the World's First Gender-Neutral Voice Technology. Dezeen. March 22. https://www.dezeen.com/2019/03/22/q-gender-neutral-voice-technology-virtue/

Materialising gender fairness through iconic language: empowering tools from and for the design community.

Valeria Bucchetti and Francesca Casnati

1 Communication design through the lens of gender

This contribution is conceived as an attempt to provide an answer, one of the several possible, to the huge issue posed by the editors of this volume regarding the meaning and the many forms through which *gender fairness* can *materialise* through design, considering in this case the *communication design* field. Wearing the 'lens of gender' from the disciplinary perspective of communication design means trying to move forward on a field that has already been partly traced by studies that – starting from Laura Mulvey's theories developed in the cinematographic sphere and, more generally, from the intersection between feminist theories and visual cultures – have historically brought to light the close link between media representations and the processes of gender construction. It is after all well-established that images constitute the *matrix of the imaginary*, recognition/misrecognition and identification, thus articulating the *self*, the subjectivity (Mulvey 1975), and how subjectivity relates to collectivity. This implies firstly considering and critically examining the domain of *visual representation* and *iconic languages* as a possible vehicle of gender representations that can shape individual and collective biographies.

The framework we live in is densely populated by 'iconic acts' that, with their message, obstruct the path towards a fair society (Bucchetti 2024: 57). To better frame the perspective from which this issue is approached, it can be useful to first mention the concept of "adaptive patriarchy" (Giolo), by which is meant a system that *relentlessly repositions the mechanisms and rhetorics of domination and control, perpetuating hierarchies, roles, and stereotypes* that hinder the path to gender fairness. In a contemporary socio-cultural context in which patriarchy seems to have improved its ability to resist and, indeed, to *adapt*, we are particularly interested in shedding light on the responsibility that designed images have in these processes and on the strategies that can be adopted to break out of the patterns and rules of patriarchy.

This issue is further nuanced by Demaria's (2019) concept of gender as a *semiotic device* that individuals assume as a component of their own identity, drawing upon the expression *en-gendering*. The en-gendering of individuals occurs when they 'adhere to the meaning effects produced by gender representations, or rather by the 'gender technologies', to use the term that Teresa de Lauretis assigned to those power devices […] within which gender models are produced and consumed' (Demaria 2019: 43, authors' translation). Among these power technologies are the media and communication artefacts which saturate our environment with visual stimuli. In this media-saturated world, we are constantly exposed to a deluge of low-quality, *bad images*.[1]

We live and act in a society that grows through images, that through images communicates, narrates itself, shows itself, distorts itself, that through images represents itself, produces its own visual stereotypes, which in turn develop fixities and prejudices, entails in fact being dropped into a flow very close to the vicious circle. A loop in which *new images* are determined in close relation to those that formed the sensibilities and mental archives of those who generated them.

Within this context, communication designers carry a significant responsibility. They should (must?) develop and equip themselves with tools to design not only in a responsible and sustainable way but also, in a proactive perspective, conceiving design a *vehicle for a fair vision* and themselves becoming *agents of change*.

The primary objective of this chapter is, through the presentation of the 'Manifesto for gender-sensitive communication' and the path that led to its definition, to reflect on the strategies and points of attention that each communication designer (and not only) should keep in mind when approaching any visual communication project, from the slides for a presentation to the design of complex systems.

2 The designers' agency and the urgency to reverse a vicious circle.

'Designing is fundamental to being human – we design, that is to say, we deliberate, plan and scheme in ways which prefigure our actions and makings… we design our world, while our world acts back on us and designs us' (Costanza-Chock 2019).

Every day we have to deal with *iconic acts* that often find their place at the bottom of the *iceberg of gender violence*[2], among the manifestations defined as 'subtle' and 'invisible' that contribute to feeding a 'system of images' that carries a sexist culture, grown according to a widespread model of *hypertrophic* communication (Bucchetti 2024: 58). This form of communication has relentlessly amplified and repeated a singular portrayal of women, to the point of fixation, reinforcing a dominant model that fails to capture the complexity and diversi-

---

1 Concept on which Valeria Bucchetti focuses in the volume *Cattive immagini* (2021), FrancoAngeli.
2 The iceberg model of gender-based violence serves as a visual framework for categorizing the various forms in which violence manifests. Expressions of violence are mapped according to two axes: *visible-invisible* and *explicit-subtle*. E.g. sexist humor, sexist advertising, and sexist language, along with forms of micro aggressions, invalidation, and invisibility, are positioned in the *invisible-subtle* category.

ty of society and the multifaceted roles that women play within it. When communication design is approached without adequate awareness, it can unwittingly replicate power dynamics that are not truly fair. The resulting design output and its perceived effects can have the power to exclude a particular social group (Levick-Parkin 2017).

Every design choice implemented by a designer can be considered a *political act*, implying a choice regarding *inclusion* or *exclusion*. Designing involves therefore an important decision: *who should/can be represented and whom one decides to represent (and in relation to whom/what)*. Designing requires recognizing one's own responsibilities and developing full awareness of what is conveyed through the designed artefacts and the impact they can have on the sociocultural context. If design culture is one of the social practices in which the representation of ways of thinking and acting, mental constructs and systems of ideas take shape, which actions and tools can we develop to promote an approach to communication design (and beyond) that gives spaces and voices to *Alterity* (Zingale 2024), deviating from the dominant model that equates masculinity with the *norm* and anyone else to the *Other*?[3]

Communication designers who do not dispose of the tools to identify their own gender biases and the forms through which biases are translated by themselves into communicative artefacts, become propulsive force in a *paradoxical system* in which models, stereotypes, commonplaces and gender roles are self-perpetuating and reinforcing. This system can be represented through the symbol of infinity (∞), that well highlights the paradox at the basis of stereotyping mechanisms: the stereotype is exploited and amplified by the media system, influencing social identity, that in turn confirms it, in a vicious circle in which the designers act as a *catalyst*, being themselves subject to cultural biases and mental schemes of which they are not always aware and which they translate into the project (Bucchetti & Casnati 2019).

At the centre is what Braidotti describes as a 'centralised data bank', which eliminates and excludes the existence, activities, practices and alternative or subordinate memories of anyone who is considered other, other than male, white, western, straight etc. A database that determines not only individual and collective biographies but also the perception of Self and the world, defining a collective and shared imaginary from which communication designers inevitably draw when it comes to producing images. Images that once in circulation will feed and consolidate that same imaginary from which they were generated in an infinite loop in which designers are both senders and addressees.

---

3 'The point here is that difference, being 'other than' or 'different from' 'Man', is actually negatively perceived as 'worth less than' 'Man'. This epistemic and symbolic exclusion is no abstraction: it translates into ruthless violence for the real-life people who happen to coincide with categories of negative difference.' Rosi Braidotti, *Post-human Feminism* (2021).

Figure 1: The paradox of the stereotype. A reinterpretation of the paradox loop of the stereotype

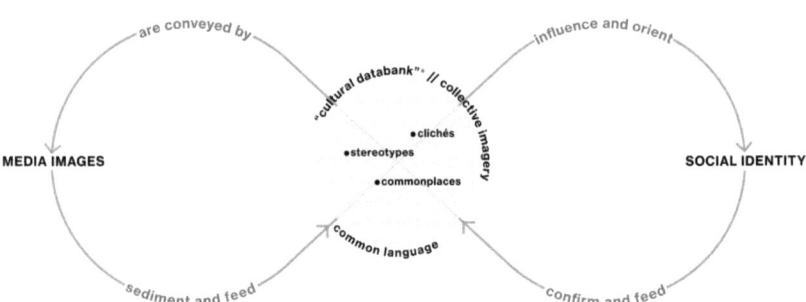

Bucchetti & Casnati, 2020: 175

Every image implicitly produces in our culture a reality effect that profoundly influences its fruition. In 'Invisible Women', Criado-Perez (2019) mentions the concept of *inertia of thought*, 'in a way, a way of not thinking', a concept that can easily be traced back to the common way in which we too often design images and artefacts: we are so familiar to the models and representational languages that surround us that we end up taking them for granted, considering them the most correct and the most effective, forgetting that they are rooted in a retrograde and androcentric model. 'Even if we [designers] have the best possible intentions, even if we use tools that are defined as *neutral* and *universal*[4], we always put our own culture and prejudices into our design projects and take a personal position, even if we don't realise it' (Fry 2017; Pater 2021; Califano 2022). It can be argued that the pervasive nature of images thus leads us to a condition similar to *habituation*: we are so accustomed to the models of (un)reality repeatedly proposed by the media, that those impossible models end up being perceived as *reality*, *normality*, the correct reference point to aspire to (Baule/Bucchetti 2012; Bucchetti 2021; Casnati 2022). Barthes in 1980 wrote with foresight: 'I had induced from the truth of the image the reality of its origin; I had confused truth and reality in one emotion' (authors' translation).

Starting from an ideal situation in which the designer has no negative intentions to denigrate or exclude a particular social group, can its *choices* really be defined as *free*[5]? How can we act to break or redirect this endless loop? Which

---

4 See Bucchetti, Valeria; Casnati, Francesca (2019) *'Icons: Normativity and Gender Inequalities'*, Phenomenology and Mind, 17, 160–172, doi.org/10.13128/pam-8034
5 Regarding *free choice*, Facchi and Giolo write: 'The exaltation of free choice as a criterion of freedom also makes it possible not to investigate traditionally oppressive practices; at times, it even prevents doing so, giving them a new legitimacy and inducing

tools can we equip ourselves with? And, as researchers and designers, which tools can we provide at the service of the community?

3   Manifesto for a gender-sensitive communication, a tool for the designers' community.

Within this outlined scenario, and with the awareness of the role that communication design can play, we have worked[6] in recent years to strengthen the tools useful for fostering self-reflective processes in this field, so that, particularly in the educational context, a process of awareness and responsibility could be undertaken to overcome, but also to counteract, the production of iconic texts with discriminatory content and their unintentional transmission. During this pathway, made up of research, networking, interdisciplinary[7] intertwining, which saw the birth of dedicated teaching[8] and multiple training opportunities, the *Manifesto for gender-sensitive communication*[9] was formalised. Through the writing and publication of this document we wish to share a declaration of intent, of principles that we commit ourselves to accept and support. It is a document that expresses a stance, fueled by the will to make a change and act on it from the disciplinary orientation of design, according to a perspective dictated by Visual Cultures.

The Manifesto, which takes the form of a website, primarily consists of three sections. Following the tradition of previous manifestos, it begins with a statement that declares 'who we are', how we identify ourselves and the community we belong to. This self-definition is crucial for immediate recognition and identification by the audience. After the 'who we are' section, the Manifesto contin-

---

one to suspend judgment on them' (Facchi & Giolo, 2020: 13. Authors' translation).

6   We refer to the work of the *dcxcg* research group – Communication design for Gender cultures – of the Design Department (Politecnico di Milano). The group is located around the intersection between communication design and gender studies. It was formed to offer a critical point of view regarding the forms of representation of gender. At the same time, the intention of supporting and developing, through research and experimental teaching, the proposal of new communication models, as well as opportunities/actions aimed at increasing sensitivity and awareness regarding gender issues in everyday life. See: http://www.dcxcg.org/.

7   This specifically refers to the active involvement of the *dcxcg* group in the *Gender Cultures Interuniversity Research Center*, established in 2013 in Milan. The Center aims to promote studies, research, and positive actions – also within the university itself – on topics related to gender cultures, using the disciplinary tools and expertise from each field involved in a multidisciplinary perspective.

8   At the Design School, Politecnico di Milano, the course 'Communication design and Gender culture' was activated and introduced in 2015 – the first of its kind in Italy –, aimed at master's degree design students.

9   See: https://www.comunicazionegendersensitive.polimi.it/.

ues with a declaration articulating and formalizing a clear standpoint. The declaration is composed by:
a) the *credo* – 'we believe that communication is a tool for inclusion and a space to build creative forms of resistance'– reaffirms the role of communication as a fundamental actor in driving processes of social innovation.
b) An appeal – 'we demand advocacy against gender inequalities, gender roles, stereotyping of identities; the abolition of gender-based hierarchies; respect for personal choices' – that concisely expresses the macro-issues that, when manifested in communicative artefacts, are amplified and consolidated. These issues revolve around the non-recognition, non-respect and denial of alterity, against which a firm stance is called for.
c) An explicit declaration of commitment and assumption of responsibility follows – 'we are committed to inclusive and diversity-friendly visual and verbal language, embracing the ten principles of gender-sensitive communication'. – This last passage of the declaration refers to the second part of the Manifesto: *the ten principles for gender-sensitive communication and the commitment to integrate them into daily practice.*

Figure 2: Screenshot of the website https://www.comunicazionegendersensitive.polimi.it/en/home-2/#statement showing the first part of the declaration.

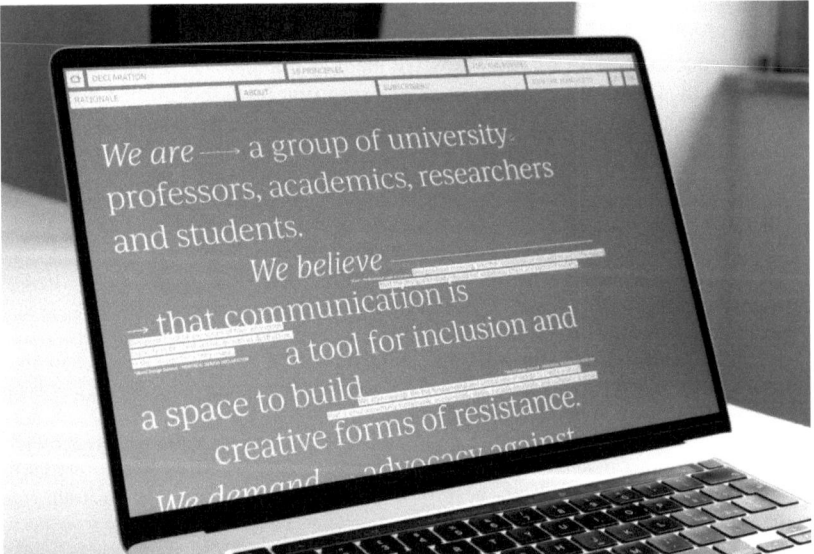

Bucchetti, Casnati, Rossi 2022

We believe the strength of this Manifesto lies indeed in its programmatic role: it synthesizes key concepts from theoretical and practical reflection into *actionable guidelines*. These concepts are distilled into ten essential principles for 'gender-sensitive' communication, presented in sequential order, and practical recommendations to guide daily actions and communicative projects toward a greater sociocultural sustainability from the point of view of *gender fairness*. The principles and points of attention are closely interconnected, resulting from a complex translation process. Initially, we identified and grouped the semantic and morphological asymmetries in images that convey gender imbalances. This led to two parallel efforts: translating these clusters into practical guidance for creating or selecting gender-sensitive images and, conversely, generalizing specific observations into the ten foundational principles. The ten principles represent essential requirements that a gender-sensitive visual and verbal language must fulfil. Each principle is anchored by a key term, accompanied by a brief explanation that clarifies its intended meaning and the perspective from which it is approached.

1. *Equal*, ensuring fair representation and visibility for individuals;
2. *Inclusive*, addressing everyone indiscriminately, countering the "male-as-default" norm;
3. *Respectful*, taking into account the diversity of identities, choices and personal orientations;
4. *Fair*, recognizing roles, skills, titles and merits without any distinction;
5. *Anti-stereotypical*, abolishing stereotypes, expressions and clichés root-ed in an asymmetrical and androcentric worldview;
6. *A-hierarchical*, rejecting forms that underlie implicit gender-based hierarchies;
7. *Non-binary*, enhancing plurality and uniqueness as opposed to male/female polarisation;
8. *Intersectional*, considering different social identities and forms of discrimination;
9. *Unconventional*, finding solutions that break with gender-based conventions;
10. *Aware*, recognizing and anticipating the impact of a message on individuals and society

The Manifesto can be therefore considered as a meeting point between theoretical study, research and practical activity. It was thought as a tool for self-reflection and guidance in daily design practice, which is why we considered it crucial to supplement it with a part that would put the focus on some *points of attention*, which we could define as 'strategies' to bypass stereotypes and *clichés* and 'transform' the effect of representations. These strategies are underpinned not only by a linguistic and critical project but also by an ethical and political one through which the social action is expressed.

4   Tips and advice for a gender-fair iconic language

Before delving into the *points of attention*, it is important to note that the Manifesto is primarily aimed at communication designers, but it is crucial to recognize that the responsibility for shaping narrative structures extends beyond professional designers. It also applies to anyone who participates in society's communicative landscape, even without formal design training. Individuals contribute to the transformation of the media system through everyday visual and textual practices – whether creating for example visual layouts in presentations, which organize text and images without specialized design skills, or engaging in social media, where producing static and moving images for posts, stories, and digital memes has become commonplace. Although their level of responsibility and involvement may differ, these 'image-makers' are active participants in the media ecosystem. This highlights the broader societal implications of visual communication and underscores the shared social responsibility inherent in our interactions with media.

The *tips and advice* (or points of attention) are intended to make explicit the virtuous behaviors inherent in the design process, as well as to exemplify the pitfalls to avoid. Therefore, they constitute a set of 'notes' intended to support the creation of visual texts[10], in line with the principles of gender-sensitive communication. The following is a summary that helps in understanding the nature of these tips, as well as their content.

Giving visibility[11] – 'The strength of the masculine order is seen in the fact that it dispenses with justification: the androcentric vision imposes itself as neutral and has no need to spell itself out in discourses aimed at legitimating it. The social order functions as an immense symbolic machine tending to ratify the mascu-

---

10 The Italian version of the Manifesto includes also a section of tips and advice for a gender-sensitive verbal language, which is the result of research and analysis of institutional documents, which provide guidelines and 'rules' for inclusive and equitable verbal language, have been reviewed and analyzed. One example is the guidelines promoted by the Ministry of Education (MIUR) in the document 'Guidelines for the Use of Administrative Language' (2018). The findings from mapping the sources allowed for the extraction of key passages, which were then adapted and, more importantly, translated from verbal language to the domain of iconic-visual language. This shift is particularly significant given the inherent slipperiness of visual language, which resists 'grammatical rules.' Such rules are easily overlooked in the process of creating a visual composition, even though seemingly minor variations that can alter the production of meaning.

11 We refer specifically to the two points outlined in the manifesto: (1) *Ensuring fair representation*. Ensure that in the selection of images – when a community or a group of subjects is represented – women and men are equally represented, in order to guarantee the quantitative representativeness of both female and male subjects. (2) *Avoid the use of the man-as-default*. Do not use images depicting only male subjects if the message is neutral or when addressing all genders indiscriminately.

line domination on which it is founded' (Bourdieu 1998: 9. Authors' translation).

The *invisibility* of the feminine is a phenomenon observed in both verbal (specifically within the Italian language) and visual languages, often justified by a supposed neutrality in expressions and representations that, in reality, embody a masculine bias. Choosing images, for example, that exclusively depict male subjects to represent an entire, diverse community does not reflect neutrality but instead creates a *male-centric representation*, effectively marginalising the feminine perspective (Bucchetti 2022) and anyone who does not fall into the category of male, white, healthy, wealthy, ...

To counteract the use of the masculine as an inclusive norm, as a presumed neutral representation – *man-as-default* or *male as norm* – and to allow the affirmation of the feminine as a subject, it is necessary first to acknowledge and explicitly recognize the presence of women through language. It is therefore crucial to "avoid the use of the man-as-default" ensuring, for example, not to use images depicting only male subjects when the message is neutral or when addressing all genders indiscriminately. Furthermore, in all the cases where a community or a group of subjects is represented, it is essential to 'ensure fair representation' by verifying that the subjects are equally represented in the selection of images, guaranteeing fair *quantitative* representativeness.

Fair-representing[12] – Numerical equity in representation must be complemented by qualitative considerations, which take into account the type of images selected, their usage modes and contexts, and their relationship with accompanying text. It is essential to question the relevance of an image within its context: *how does the image relate to the surrounding context? How does it relate to the surrounding content? What meaning does it add? Why was it selected?* Ensuring that images are relevant to their context is a crucial step in avoiding discriminatory portrayals that confine female subjects to merely decorative or visually appealing roles, objectifying woman. This practice is so pervasive that the Italian term '*grechina*' – with no male equivalent – has emerged to describe cases where images of women are used solely for ornamental purposes, without any substantive link to the content or context.

Empowering[13] – In representations involving both male and female figures,

---

12 (3) *Verify the relevance of the images to their context.* Ensure that the way subjects are represented is relevant and consistent with the context. For example, avoid the use of female figures for mere decorative and attractive purposes.

13 (4) *Ensure a non-discriminatory representation of roles.* Promote the representation of the multiplicity of roles, for example by choosing images depicting women and men in unconventional roles and professions so as not to feed clichés, making sure to include, when possible, representations of women in top positions. (5) *Foster forms of representation that do not imply gender-based hierarchies.* Do not use depictions that implicitly convey hierarchical relationships of women's inferiority to men. The main elements to be checked in the case of images depicting more than one subject concern:

there is a frequent tendency toward hierarchical depictions that, whether consciously or unconsciously, subordinate women to men. This phenomenon is observed for example in pictogrammatic systems (Bucchetti/Casnati 2019) that usually presume to be *universal*, but it crosses all areas of visual communication. Based on these observations, a point of attention on visual hierarchies was developed, urging consideration of «hierarchical relationships and those parameters that lead the viewer to perceive, at varying levels of awareness, a subordinate relationship of women to men» (Bucchetti/Casnati 2019: 166). Proactively, this guideline encourages forms of representation that avoid gender-based hierarchies, with attention to the *relationships among depicted subjects in terms of quantity, spatial arrangement, scale, and action*.

In group depictions, for instance, an equal number of female and male figures should be represented (quantitative balance); female figures should not consistently be placed in the background or behind male figures (spatial arrangement); female figures should not be depicted as smaller than male figures without reason, especially in pictogrammatic languages (scale balance); and there should be no imbalance of active and passive roles assigned by gender.

A more equitable portrayal of women and men also requires 'non-discriminatory representation of roles.' This guideline draws attention to the impact of gender roles, advocating for diversity in the selection of images that portray women and men in non-stereotypical roles and professions, ensuring, when possible, that women are represented in leadership positions.

Unveiling the plurality[14] – Defining femininity and masculinity as two strict-

---

[a] QUANTITATIVE BALANCE: refers to the numerical representativeness of women and men (e.g. in depictions of groups, check that there is an equal number of female and male subjects); [B] SPATIAL RELATIONSHIPS: refers to the positioning of subjects in space (e.g. take care that when depicting groups or couples, female subjects are not always in the background or 'behind' the male ones); [C] DIMENSIONAL RATIOS: refers to the depiction of female subjects that are dimensionally smaller than male subjects (e.g. when using pictographic figures of men and women, ensure that there are no unjustified dimensional dissimilarities); [D] ACTION PERFORMED: activity and passivity of the subjects depicted. It concerns the roles and actions performed by the subjects so that there is no prevalence of passive/active behaviours in relation to gender.

14 (6) *Avoid reinforcing dominant aesthetic ideals*. Give preference to images whose subjects have heterogeneous physicality and traits, in order not to disseminate standardised and idealised images of women and men. When selecting images, give more importance to the role of the subjects rather than their appearance. (7) *Avoid depicting women and men in ways that reinforce their status quo*. Consider, for example, the elements characterising the subjects within an image – posture, expressions, gestures, attitudes and clothing – as potential vectors of sexist social models. From the opposite perspective, these elements can be positively exploited to convey values of fairness and inclusion. (8) *Promote the use of heterogeneous and non-stereotypical colour palettes*. Choose colour palettes that are not polarised according to the canons: pink=female/blue=male. If it

ly dichotomous concepts, understood primarily through contrast and difference (Zingale 2012), inevitably leads to the construction of binary and polarized models of representation that oversimplify and erase their inherent complexity, nuances, and ambiguities. Yet, the concept of Alterity is far broader and dynamic, encompassing a fluid understanding in which everyone can be viewed as both Self and Other in relation to themselves and to what is different from them. Reducing this complexity to a limited set of representational models results in a partial, distorted, and often discriminatory portrayal of reality.

Design practice must continually engage with this complexity, reflecting the layered nature of reality while affirming the value, importance, and beauty of plurality.

In practical terms, designers should strive to introduce varied subjects and imagery that resist the rigidity of stereotyped and overused representational models. How does this translate into actionable steps?

In formulating the latest recommendations, we focused on offering guidance that encourages designers to experiment with alternative models and to move beyond the representational *clichés* that can form a 'comfort zone'. This task involves balancing the need to offer precise and clear suggestions while avoiding overly prescriptive instructions. Practically, this involves selecting images that feature diverse physicalities and characteristics, avoiding the dissemination of standardized and idealized depictions of both women and men. In this spirit, it is recommended to 'avoid reinforcing dominant aesthetic ideals'. Moreover, to 'challenge portrayals that reinforce the status quo', designers should consider elements such as posture, expression, gesture, attitude, and clothing as potential carriers of gendered social expectations. By reimagining and transforming these elements, designers can use them positively to convey values of equity and inclusion.

Fostering and representing plurality also requires thoughtful choices in colour and symbolic representation. It is recommended to «promote the use of diverse and non-stereotypical colour palettes», selecting hues that do not conform to traditional gender associations, such as pink for females and blue for males. When it is necessary to differentiate or designate genders through colour, consider palettes that break away from the conventional pink/blue codes. Furthermore, in symbolic depictions related to gender, it is advisable to 'opt for images that avoid visual clichés', steering clear of stereotypical symbols, such as lipstick or high-heeled shoes to represent women, or a tie to represent men.

The points of attention aim to provide concrete support for taking a stance, with the hope that they can be internalised to the extent of be-coming almost automatic, prompting the right question at the right time in every design path, thus

---

is necessary to identify or mark the two genders chromatically, choose palettes that do not respond to conventional pink/blue codes. (9) *Opt for images that move away from visual clichés.* When using symbolic depictions in referring to gender, avoid stereotypical associations such as, for example, lipstick or high-heeled shoes to designate the female gender or a tie for the male gender.

avoiding the trap of stereotypes. The Manifesto and its points of attention appeal to the social responsibility of designers and all those involved in the field of communication design. They provide practical tools that can be effectively integrated into daily practices and translate into a tangible commitment to promoting forms of representation that go beyond the deeply rooted sexist remnants in visual and verbal language. This is achieved through an inclusive, gender-sensitive and equal language that embraces plurality and fairness as its expressive form.

5 Conclusion

Addressing gender fairness through iconic languages by drafting a manifesto of intentions and programmatic points of attention posed a significant challenge.

The manifesto format compels authors to distil intentions and ideas, carefully selecting the clearest, most effective words to convey the message with concision, immediacy, and impact. This format also permits and even demands an assertive tone, stepping away from the caution that typically characterises scientific discourse, to express a firm and unambiguous stance that encourages critical reflection, sometimes through confrontation. In academic contexts, creating a manifesto means more than acknowledging the urgency of an issue; it involves taking a declared position and creating a tool designed to spark dialogue, confrontation, and reflection. As Olivia Lucca Fraser, a member of the group Laboria Cubonik, which drafted *The Xenofeminist Manifesto*, remarked, 'the whole point of writing something like [a manifesto] is to try to reshape the discursive chessboard, at least in some small but structural way, and not just to move the existing pieces around' (2016). The main difficulty faced was to find a way to tackle an extraordinarily complex and current issue, one that is still wide open to debate and reflection, while successfully summarizing the crucial issues without generalising or trivialising the subject matter and effectively conveying it through the distinctive assertive tone and concise writing that characterise the manifesto format. This distinctive, assertive, and succinct style defines the Manifesto's value as well as its limitations. Summarising inherently requires choices about what to include or omit, a process that can leave behind certain nuances. Yet this clarity and brevity are essential to achieving effective, immediate communication.

Closely related to this challenge was the task of finding the right tone, specificity, and prescriptiveness for the points of attention, offering sufficient guidance while allowing room for individual interpretation and alignment with the Manifesto's goals. These needs led to focusing the Gender-Sensitive Communication Manifesto's stance and operational principles on the non-representation/under-representation/misrepresentation of women.

With its strengths and potential for impact, the Manifesto is a valuable tool for articulating and sharing a critical stance. Rather than a final or definitive product, it serves as a starting point to inspire reflection, foster dialogue, encourage critical thinking, and push boundaries. The Manifesto can and should function as a platform for reflection, inviting collaboration across diverse professional backgrounds and enriching perspectives. An illustrative example of this idea is the 2020 re-edition of the *First Things First Manifesto*. Its open-access, editable format online empowers designers and subscribers not only to endorse it but also to actively participate in its evolution, adding new layers of insight and incorporating fresh awareness from their professional practice.

Beyond promoting collaboration and integrating expertise from various fields, it is crucial to consider the potential evolution of the Manifesto as a living document, nurturing the growth of this project. This involves for instance exploring diverse formats to facilitate wider dissemination and easier sharing, as well as developing practical tools to enhance its applicability. The Manifesto's potential for growth exists on multiple levels. Firstly, inherent to the nature of the Manifesto is the capacity for expansion and increased participation; we hope it can, in its own way, generate a ripple effect, gradually influencing and permeating the design community and beyond.

From a research and experimental standpoint, the Manifesto can be useful across several dimensions. Its focal points can be adopted and transformed into key criteria for phenomenological observation. These focal points could serve as parameters for evaluation and analysis, helping to examine and document specific media contexts. This would support the ongoing work of the *dcxcg* research group, which has been critically documenting and analysing the current media landscape and its discriminatory practices over the years. Moreover, by shifting perspective, it is also possible to envision these focal points being applied positively and proactively – both in educational settings and within experimental design practices. This approach could lead to the development of solutions and strategies aimed at defining alternative languages that align with principles of gender fairness and plurality.

References

Arruzza, C./Bhattacharya, T./Fraser, N., (2019). *Feminism for a 99%: a manifesto*. London, Verso.
Baule, G./Bucchetti, V. (eds.) (2012). *Anticorpi Comunicativi. Progettare per la comunicazione di genere*. Milano, FrancoAngeli.
Bourdieu, P., (1998). *Il dominio maschile*, Feltrinelli, Trans It. (1998).
Braidotti, R., (2021). *Post-human Feminism*. Camebridge: Polity.
Bucchetti, V., (2021). *Cattive immagini. Design della comunicazione, grammatiche e parità di genere*. Franco Angeli.

Bucchetti, V., Casnati, F., Rossi, M., (2022). "Manifesto for a Gender-Sensitive Communication. From the Communication Design Perspective". https://www.comunicazionegendersensitive.polimi.it/en/home-2/#statement.

Bucchetti, V./Casnati, F., (2022). "Communication design to foster gender equality: Research and experimentation in the educational field". In: Skjærven, A./ Maureen Fordham, M., (eds.) – Gender and the Sustainable Development Goals Infrastructure, Empowerment and Education. London: Routledge.

Bucchetti, V./Casnati, F., (ed.), (2022). *Tracce di iper-in-visibilità: Rappresentazione e disparità di genere: uno sguardo sulla quotidianità.* FrancoAngeli.

Bucchetti, V./Casnati, F., (2020). Icons: Normativity and Gender Inequalities. In: Bojanić S., Loddo O.G., Zubčić M., (ed.), *Phenomenology and Mind*, (17). 160–172.https://doi.org/10.13128/pam-8034

Bucchetti V., Casnati F. (2020). The role of women in technologies according to the media. How communication design can react. In: Ban, S., Guida, F. (edited by), PAD #19 COMMUNICATION DESIGN APART
ISSN 1972-7887

Capecchi, S., (2018). *La comunicazione di genere. Prospettive teoriche e buone pratiche.* Roma, Carocci.

Casnati, F./Rossi, M., (2024). 'The recognition of the Other through (iconic) language. Gender-sensitive practices and advice from and for communication design'. In Zingale, S. (ed.), Design meets alterity. FrancoAngeli, Open access catalog, Milano.

Costanza-Chock, S., (2020). *Design Justice. Community-led practices to build the worlds we need.* Camebridge: MIT Press.

Criado-Perez, C., (2019). *Invisible Women: Exposing Data Bias in a World Designed for Men.* NY: Random House.

De Lauretis, T., (1987). *Technologies of Gender. Essays on Theory, Film and Fiction.* Bloomington, Indiana University Press.

Demaria, C., (2019). *Teorie di genere. Femminismi e semiotica.* Bompiani Campo Aperto.

Frichot, H., (2016). *How to make yourself a Feminist Design Power Tool.* AADR.

Goffman, E., (1987). *Gender Advertisements.* NY: Harper & Row.

Laboria Kubonics, (2018). *The Xenofeminist Manifesto. A politics for alienation.* London/NY: Verso Books.

Levick-parkin, M., (2017). "The values of being in design: Towards a feminist design ontology". *GENDER : Zeitschrift fur Geschlecht, Kultur und Gesellschaft*, 9 (3), 11–25.

Mulvey, L., (2019). Afterimages: On Cinema, Women and Changing Times. London: Reaktion books.

Zingale, S., (2022). *Design e alterità. Conoscere l'altro e pensare il possibile.* FrancoAngeli.

Why Representation Matters: Reclaiming Space – The Evolution of Women in Tech

Franziska Beckert

Part of the content provided in this contribution originates from my master thesis, which I wrote before starting my career in the German tech industry. To understand current inequalities in the tech scene, it is helpful to examine the historical context and the circumstances under which the tech industry became one of the most male dominated industries in the industrialised countries of the northern hemisphere. It will also help to illustrate that gender associations of industries are indeed changeable (Abbate 2012: 4). As a part of my research, I also conducted over 20 interviews with female high-school students, female programmers, and men and women who are executives in the tech industry. These findings, combined with my own lived experience as a woman in tech, shed light on the barriers women face when considering a career in tech but also on the measures that could help increase female participation in tech.

Figure 1: ENIAC programming with telephone, Betty Jean Jennings Bartik (left)

University Archives and Records Center/University of Pennsylvania

Computer science is the youngest discipline among the STEM subjects; it first became relevant during World War II. At that time, approximately 25% of programmers were women (Abbate 2012: 18). This was partly due to men being recruited into the military, but also because the industry was new and not yet associated with a particular gender. Hardware development was considered more significant than the actual programming during that era. Thus, men focused on hardware development and women on software. In those days being a programmer was seen as similar to being a telephone operator, which was overwhelmingly executed by women (see figure 1) (Ensmenger 2010: 121f.).

One of the earliest electronic computers, the ENIAC, had its software primarily developed by women. In 1944, Grace Hopper, one of the most well-known early programming pioneers, participated in the programming of the Mark I. This computer was significant because it contributed to the development of the American atomic bomb. Hopper invented the compiler and contributed to the evolution of the COBOL programming language (Chang 2018: 17).

Post World War II, there was an explosion of workforce demand in the private computer sector. Between 1960 and 1970, the number of computer employees in the USA multiplied by twenty, around 25% were women. (U.S. Department of Commerce, 1985) Because of the high demand, women were targeted as well, as they were considered 'cost-effective' and 'loyal' (Abbate 2012: 65). Traits like patience, empathy, attention to detail, and communication skills were viewed as a foundation to become a successful programmer. A good example of this way of thinking can be found in the Cosmopolitan article 'The Computer Girl' from 1967 (Mandel, 1967). Here, programming was portrayed as a feminine activity with phrases such as '[...] and if it doesn't sound like women's work – well, it just is' (Mandel 1967: 52) and the lucrative salaries it offered were highlighted. In the article Grace Hopper compared programming to preparing dinner, claiming women were natural programmers. Despite these efforts to feminise programming in order to attract inexpensive labour, women's successes were often masculinised. For instance, Grace Hopper became the first 'man of the year award' winner in 1969 (Ensmenger 2010: 117). Another quote illustrating this contradiction is from her former supervisor Howard Aiken from Harvard University who said 'Grace was a good man' (Isaacson 2020).

The advancing masculinisation of professions correlates with an increasing professionalisation, because professionalism is commonly seen as a masculine trade. This can be observed in the field of computer science as well. As early as the mid-1960s, a good 80 percent of companies relied on aptitude tests[1] to recruit their employees. These aptitude tests heavily relied on mathematical skills and therefore favoured men due to easier access to higher education (Ensmenger

---

1 Since the 1920s it was known that aptitude tests were not scientifically significant. Despite this information, the tests were used for recruiting in the computer industry up until the 1980s. (Cannon & Perry, 1966, P. 61–82)

2010: 125ff.). In 1966, the 'Programmer Scale' developed by psychologists Cannon & Perry aimed to identify individuals who were mathematically skilled and had a 'disinterest in people'. They concluded 'Programmers dislike activities involving close personal interaction. They prefer to work with things rather than people' (Cannon & Perry, 1966: 61–82). This widespread image of the 'ideal type of programmer' developed into a 'self-fulfilling prophecy'. From this idolized picture of a programmer the stereotype of the socially incompetent, mathematically gifted programmer ('computer nerd'), typically depicted as male and young arose (Ensmenger 2010: 129). Until today, this stereotype continues to influence the culture in the tech industry, with well-known success stories of young, white men who built tech giants like Facebook, Google or Amazon in a garage.

In this narrative, women rarely play a significant role; today the actual participation of women differs from country to country significantly (see figure 2). In Europe, countries like Germany, the Netherlands or the UK, rank low concerning female participation with around 15% in the tech industry. In contrast, Eastern European countries like Bulgaria have higher female participation, about 30%, followed by Romania, Lithuania, and Latvia.

Figure 2: Country selection of female participation [%] in the teach industry 2018

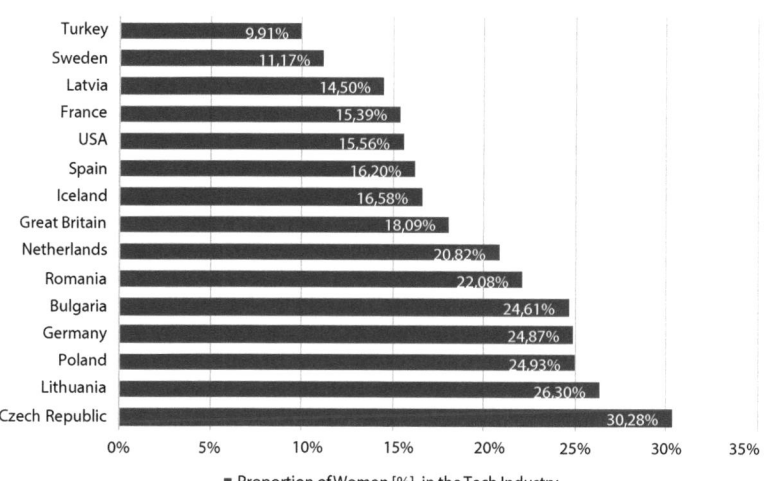

Honeypot, 2018

There are many factors which influence female participation in an industry. Female participation in former Soviet countries is significantly higher than in e.g. former West Germany. This is a clear indicator that female participation is driven by history and social norms. A great example for changeability is Germany. After the reunification of Germany in 1989, the percentage of women in computer science at the East German Technical University of Rostock fell from about 65% to the West German average of 15% within a few years (see figure 3) (Schinzel 2004).

Figure 3: Female Participation [%] in Computer Science at the Technical University of Rostock

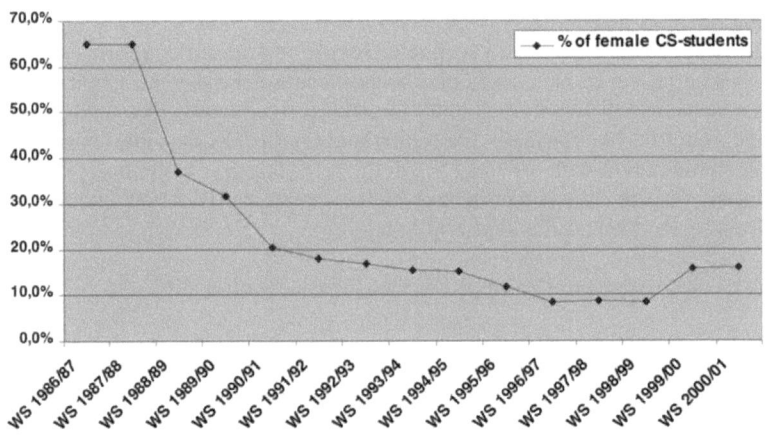

Schinzel 2004

Recent years have seen little change in the gender pay gap and female participation. However, female participation in interdisciplinary fields like medical informatics or bioinformatics is higher, with 40-50% of bachelor's graduates are women and 40% in master's programs.

It's also important to note that women leave the tech industry at twice the rate of men (Chang 2018: 7). This might also be influenced by the fact that, like in many industries, the tech industry also has a wage discrepancy between men and women. For instance, in 2018 the unadjusted gender pay gap in the German tech industry was at 25%, compared to the national cross-industry average of 20% (Honeypot 2018) – Germany ranks low compared to other countries. The European cross-industry average gender pay gap is at 16,1 percent (Reisin 2019: Statistisches Bundesamt, 2017).

Figure 4: Country selection to compare the gender pay gap [%] in the tech industry

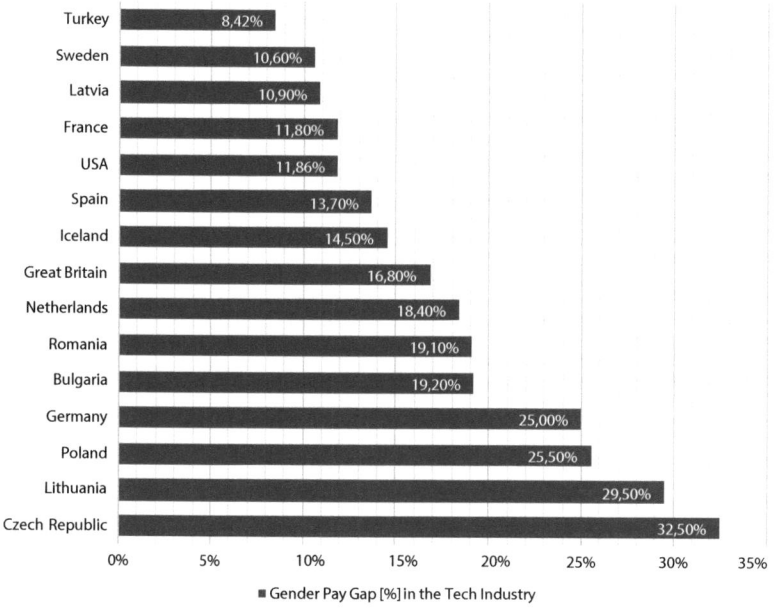

Honeypot, 2018

This raises the question of 'what measures could be taken to attract more female talent to the tech industry?'

What has to change?

First, I would like to dismantle the common stereotype that the core skill needed for programming is mathematics. In a business setting, what generally separates the good programmers from the great are interpersonal skills, such as communication and teamwork, along with problem-solving abilities, deep product understanding, creativity, and empathy.

Before I met people who worked in tech, I had little idea about the working conditions, salaries or specific job opportunities that tech has to offer. I found a similar information gap in my interviews with the high school students. It has also become clear that there is a massive need for action at an educational policy level: school graduates need to be better educated about programming and its areas of application. Information technology basics should be better integrated into the everyday school life of young people. At least in Germany, computer science is not a mandatory subject in school, even though teenagers are surrounded by tech most of their day, be it on social media platforms (TikTok, Instagram or X), or while online shopping. This is a missed opportunity to incorporate real-world applications of computer science and technology into school curriculums. A curriculum focused on these topics could increase interest, especially if this is done in an interdisciplinary manner, combining technology with other fields, such as business, art or psychology. I strongly believe that giving tech more 'range' and showcasing its versatility would encourages more individuals to consider a career in it. Professions like product management, UX design or graphic design are prime examples of such interdisciplinary fields that don't require a traditional computer science degree. I, like many others, didn't study computer science and still found a career in tech as a product manager. Product management is a profession as diverse as the products that are being managed – if you put two random product managers in a room, the chances of them having very different day to day work is extremely high.

From my personal experience and backed up through my research, women in tech face gender-specific challenges due to a lack of diversity, including assumptions about their competence and a scarcity of role models. This lack of representation makes it difficult for young women to envision a career in tech. Therefore, building a community where peers can share experiences and challenges is crucial for me and many women in this industry. This support network helps tackle the 'only woman in the room' problem by providing a space for reality checks. For example, 'Did anyone else find it weird and inappropriate that the keynote speaker used a picture of a woman in a bikini to illustrate his point?'

Another very concrete example for gender specific challenges in tech, as mentioned above, is the gender pay gap. To counteract gender pay gap issues, I think salary structures need to be transparent: everyone should be able to view the salary bands for all roles within a company. Wages outside of the salary band should not be possible. I believe such compensation systems neutralize potential differences that could arise because women often undervalue themselves and their work and ask for 20-30% less salary than men. Clearly defined role profiles with outlined expectations can be helpful. Regular performance reviews, where performance is measured against the requirements described in the role profile, should be linked to salary adjustments.

But addressing the issue holistically requires a societal commitment beyond just policy, community or education; corporations must make a clear commitment to supporting women in professional areas. Diversity and inclusion is often one of the first things companies stop paying attention to when the economic situation becomes challenging. Many companies seemingly still haven't understood that focusing their hiring efforts on women unlocks a huge candidate pool, which is an economic advantage in times of skilled labour shortage. By hiring women, companies generate more revenue. There is plenty of evidence that gender diversity, especially in senior management positions, increases a company's profitability by 3–8 percent (Christiansen et al. 2016).

Some companies have already taken specific actions to increase the proportion of women in technical professions, such as women-specific job advertisements, direct access to graduate pools, leadership development, and mentoring programs. But companies must adopt a zero-tolerance policy against toxic behaviour, which is often prevalent in the tech-industry, to keep women in the industry.

CEOs, who are predominantly male, need to scrutinize their hiring practices for top positions. They should demand from headhunters, commonly used to fill these positions, to find a female candidate for every male candidate. Furthermore, seemingly small things like having female keynote speakers as well as male ones at company events, makes a difference to female staff. Women are more likely to stay in a job and with a company when they feel represented, taken seriously and valued. Once a certain level of female participation is exceeded (around 30%), companies will have to invest less resources into their diverse hiring efforts and the women working at the company will automatically recruit more women. It makes a huge difference when one goes through a job interview process and meets lots of women working in technical roles. It makes them more likely to consider this employment opportunity because the environment is most likely welcoming to women.

More balanced and equal participation in the industry is desirable because evidence shows that a male-dominated tech world often leads to a one-sided perspective in programming, which affects how software is developed and the types of problems that are perceived and prioritised. This imbalance can result in the development of products that do not only not adequately address the needs of a diverse user base, but also potentially overlook or misunderstand the experiences of women and other underrepresented groups. For example, health apps might initially fail to include features specific to women's health, or voice recognition systems may struggle to accurately process female voices. Such biases can lead to technology that perpetuates inequality and limits the effectiveness of solutions. Furthermore, a lack of diversity in tech teams can stifle innovation, as diverse perspectives are crucial for creative problem-solving and developing inclusive products that serve a broader audience. Therefore, inspiring more women to enter the tech industry is not just about increasing female participation; it's about driving a broader societal change. We need to cultivate awareness of gender diversity and foster a profound mutual understanding where qualities are not judged based on gender associations. For example, men lacking empathy or communication skills shouldn't be excused by their gender, just as women shouldn't be expected to be great communicators or more empathetic due to their gender. Career choice, success, and prosperity must be independent of gender identity. The tech industry must reflect on who will shape the world of tomorrow and with what skills they will do so.

If an industry can transition from higher to lower female participation, like we saw in the early days of computer science, it can also transition back. It is up to us to steer this change. Despite the challenges, I encourage women to consider a career in tech. Like many industries, tech has areas that need improvement, but it also offers numerous advantages. Often working hours are flexible, the salaries are comparatively high and the problems one gets to work on are hard and interesting. It is very possible to find companies that hire excellent talent, including other women and have an awareness of the gender specific challenges. I chose tech over continuing my career in academia and 5 years later I certainly don't regret my choice. Over the course of my career I have found like-minded people who see the issues that are created when an industry so powerful is run only by men. Tech companies need to deal empathetically with human problems and human behaviour. Increasing the participation of women not only improves the work atmosphere, it ultimately leads to better products being built (over 50% of the world's population are women. It might be a good and lucrative idea to include them in the development of any product). People of all genders are needed to solve the complex and multifaceted problems of today and the future.

References

Abbate, J. (2012). *Recoding Gender – Women's Changing Participation in Somputing.* Cambridge, Massachusetts & London, England: The MIT Press.

Cannon, W./ Perry, D. (1966). *A Vocational Interest Scale for Computer Programmers.* SIGCPR, S. 61–82

Chang, E. (2018). *BROTOPIA – Breaking Up the Boys' Club of Silicon Valley.* New York: Portfolio/Penguin.

Christiansen, L./ Lin, H./Pereira, J./Topalova, P./ Turk, R. (2016). *Gender Diversity in Senior Positions and Firm Performance: Evidence from Europe .* Retrieved 25.09.2020 IMF: https://www.imf.org/external/pubs/ft/wp/2016/wp1650.pdf

Ensmenger, N. (2010). *Making Programming Masculine.* In Gender Codes - Why Women Are Leaving Computing. IEEE Computer Society. Hoboken, New Jersey, USA, Misa, Thomas J. (ed.): John Wiley & Sons, Inc.115–141

Honeypot. (2018). *2018 Women in Tech Index.* Retrieved 25.09.2020 https://www.honeypot.io/women-in-tech-2018/

Isaacson, W. (2020). *The Harvard Garzette.* Von Grace Hopper, computing pioneer: https://news.harvard.edu/gazette/story/2014/12/grace-hopper-computing-pioneer/

Mandel, L. (1967). The Computer Girls. *Cosmopolitan.* Retrieved 25.09.2020 Cosmopolitan: https://boingboing.net/2015/07/31/the-computer-girls-1967-c.html

Reisin, A. (2019). *Tagesschau - Wie hoch ist der Gender Pay Gap wirklich?* Retrieved 25.09.2020 von https://www.tagesschau.de/faktenfinder/inland/gender-paygap-103.html

Schinzel, B. (2004). *Kulturunterschiede beim Frauenanteil im Informatik-Studium. Teil II: Informatik in Deutschland.* Retrieved 25.09.2020 von http://mod.iig.uni-freiburg.de/cms/fileadmin/publikationen/online-publikationen/Informatik.Frauen.Deutschland.pdf

Statistisches Bundesamt. (2017). *Destatis.* Retrieved 25.09.2020 https://www.destatis.de/DE/Presse/Pressemitteilungen/2018/03/PD18_099_621.html

U.S. Army Photo. (1945–1947). *I Programmer.* Retrieved 25.09.2020, https://www.i-programmer.info/history/people/341-eckert-and-mauchley-and-eniac.html?start=1

U.S. Army Photo. (1945–1947). *I Programmer.* Retrieved 25.09.2020, https://www.i-programmer.info/history/people/341-eckert-and-mauchley-and-eniac.html?start=1

U.S. Army Photo. (ca. 1945–1947). *U.S. Army Research Laboratory.* Retrieved 25.09.2020 https://ftp.arl.army.mil/ftp/historic-computers/gif/eniac7.gif

U.S. Department of Commerce, B. o. (1985). *Statistical Abstract of the United States.* Washington D.C.: U.S. Gouvernment Printing Office.

Idle Uses and Body Comfort: Redesigning the Campus of the largest University in Argentina.

Griselda Flesler and Carolina Spataro

Abstract: This article[1] examines the desires and demands of students and teachers at the University of Buenos Aires Campus regarding the need for places for leisure and rest. A campus that was designed – with the functionalist criteria of the Modern Movement – to study and work, demands for other 'non-productive' uses. Based on a survey conducted in 2020 that investigated the sensations generated by different spaces on the Campus, we focused on those that demand an architecture that is sensitive to the needs of the body. We link this with some projects about university space, designed by students of the FADU's seminar 'Design and Gender Studies'. At the end of the article we propose recommendations -from the survey's findings- with the purpose of providing tools to university management to materialise fairness through design while offering valuable insights into prospective opportunities.

---

1 The research for this article stems from two research projects directed by Rafael Blanco, Griselda Flesler, and Carolina Spataro. The first is 'Demandas feministas, disidencia sexual y universidad: Transformaciones recientes en los saberes, los espacios y la sociabilidad cotidiana en la Universidad de Buenos Aires' at the Gino Germani Institute of the University of Buenos Aires. The second, at the GDS Program at Carleton University, Canada, is 'Re/designing the University of Buenos Aires campus to be gender inclusive in Argentina.'

Introduction

Trained in the philosophical context of Western metaphysical dualism, many of us have accepted the notion that there is a split between the body and the mind. Believing this, individuals enter the classroom to teach as though only the mind is present, and not the body. — bell hooks, 1994

Figure 1: University of Buenos Aires Campus.

Photo: Alejandro Goldemberg. Source: CPAU, 2011.

The aim of this article is to analyse how the design and implementation of feminist public policies on the campus of the University of Buenos Aires (UBA) enable demands that make our bodies, their needs and desires visible. A campus that was designed – with the functionalist criteria of the Modern Movement – to study and work, is demanded for other "non-productive" uses.

Argentina has a long tradition of feminist movements (Barrancos, 2007), which has become more visible in recent years. The current article is framed in the context of this massification, starting with the demonstration held in June 2015, organised by the Ni una Menos (Not one woman less) movement[2]. These mass marches across the country revealed a collective frustration around gender-based violence and the demand for its resolution. In the area of higher edu-

---

2 In 2015, the femicide of Chiara Páez, a 14-year-old who was pregnant when she was murdered by her boyfriend, led women to plan 'Ni una menos'. Women gathered at squares all across the country, though the largest rally took place in front of the Argentine Congress in the city of Buenos Aires. More information is available at https://niunamenos.org.ar/.

cation, this collective anger translated into the implementation of different gender policies in universities.

The UBA's new gender policies –particularly, spatial reconfigurations– set off debates and conflicts between institutional actors regarding the need for these transformations. For instance, the creation of offices for reporting incidents and questions of its characteristics (whether it should be soundproof, visible but not exposed, etc.) became part of the discussions and challenges faced by different administrations. In addition to the debates and conflicts, there was a strong affective stance associated with these transformations that ranged from joy to discomfort and pride (Blanco et al. 2021).

Against this backdrop, our article addresses the theoretical tradition that has been concerned with linking space with emotions, what Joyce Davidson, Liz Bondi and Mick Smith (2006) have termed *'Emotional Geographies'*. As Zaragocin and Caretta describe, 'This focus was the result of a progression of the critique of feminist epistemology toward the keystone of Western positivistic science grounded on the Cartesian dualist assumption that rationality is distinct from and superior to emotions. On the contrary, feminist geographers study bodies and emotion to proactively disrupt a long history of research and knowledge produced as objective and disembodied.' (2021:1505). Simultaneously, authors like Sara Ahmed and Lauren Berlant offered a fertile ground for this type of inquiry by analysing emotions not as psychological states but as social and cultural practices.

The case study is the University of Buenos Aires (UBA), which celebrated its bicentennial in 2021. With over 310,000 undergrads, 10,000 graduate students, 28,000 professors, and 13,000 administrative and maintenance workers, it is Argentina's largest higher education institution. Due to the quality education it provides, it is also one of the most important and prestigious universities in Latin America and worldwide.[3] The university government is tripartite, with representation of professors, alumni, and students, and it is public and tuition-free, with no admittance restrictions. The socioeconomic status of students is thus highly diverse and students tend to be very involved and politically active (Carli, 2022).

As noted in earlier works (Blanco et al., 2021), since 2015 the university administration has introduced institutional strategies targeting gender relations in day-to-day interactions at the university and in the way the campus itself is inhabited. In this regard, this article will focus specifically on spatial reconfigurations at the School of Architecture, Design and Urbanism (FADU, its Spanish acronym), exploring perceptions on how these spaces are experienced by those who study and teach design. Degree programs at FADU include Architecture, Graphic Design, Industrial Design, Landscape Design, Clothing Design, Fabric Design, and Image and Sound Design, in addition to a vast offering of graduate

---

3 https://www.topuniversities.com/universities/universidad-de-buenos-aires-uba

degree programs.[4] The school has one of the largest populations within UBA, with some 27,000 students, 3,500 professors, and 450 administrative and maintenance workers.[5] Another reason for focusing on this particular school is that in 2017, it created a Gender Office that has since introduced a range of policies.[6] Responding to reports of harassment, launching awareness campaigns, and producing data on situations of gender violence are key actions taken since the office opened.[7] Other initiatives included training courses on gender perspectives for students, professors, administrative and other workers. But the main reason for choosing FADU was that this School stands out from other higher education institutions in its early interventions to create or adapt facilities from a gender-inclusive perspective, like gender neutral bathrooms, breastfeeding rooms, care and recreation spaces for children of faculty staff and students, spaces available to make complaints privately, etc.

The quantitative and qualitative data that informed the research comes from Spaces and Daily Life on the UBA Campus, a survey of FADU students, professors and administrative personnel at the School of Architecture, Design, and Urbanism in November 2020. The 35 questions explored the emotions survey-takers experienced in everyday places at the university like classrooms, hallways, and outdoor spaces, along with the new spaces created in recent years, like the all-gender bathroom, lactation rooms, etc.

In this article, the first section offers the methodological approach and characteristics of the survey. The second section focuses on a key finding of the research: the demand for on-campus spots designed for rest and leisure. Although the survey had the objective of studying the link between space and emotions in a context of institutionalisation of gender policies, an emergent from the fieldwork indicated that the main demand had to do with leisure spaces. Finally, the third section presents some projects designed by students of the FADU's seminar 'Design and Gender Studies',

Quantitative, qualitative and design analysis

In order to respond to the research questions, the Spaces and Daily Life on the UBA Campus survey was conducted.[8] Designed between September and October 2020, the Survey Monkey survey was available online on November 1-25, 2020. A total of 1,401 people responded to the survey, representing 5.6% of the popu-

---

4   https://www.fadu.uba.ar/
5   Data from FADU-UBA, 2021.
6   For more on the UBA Gender Offices, see Flesler et al. (2020), and Flesler and Thus (2022).
7   For research into the creation of data on gender violence at UBA, see Azparren et al. (2022).
8   The full survey results are available in Spanish at: https://dyegblog.wordpress.com/extension-y-transferencias/

lation. In terms of the profile of respondents, the majority were students identifying as cisgender women under age 24 who began studying or working on campus after 2015.

The survey included 35 questions that explored the emotions elicited in a list of 19 places on campus. The sites explored in the study included a) gendered spaces, associated with practices differentiated by gender like caretaking, bathrooms (both gendered and all-gender) and places for reporting sexist violence; b) educational spaces, those associated with learning, teaching and research; c) outdoor spaces, meeting spaces and traffic areas where students at FADU interact or pass through on a daily basis; and d) administrative areas, i.e., offices and other spaces generally reserved for administrative staff, professors and student government representatives. The emotions that survey takers could choose from included joy, sadness, pride, shame, comfort, discomfort, safety, fear, pleasure, disgust, indifference, love and hate. 'Don't know' was also listed as a response.

The survey consisted almost entirely of simple, multiple-choice questions. It also included questions on informed consent, role at the institution, first year at the institution, time of day most frequently spent at the university, type of transport most commonly used to get to campus, gender and sexual orientation. Three open questions were included at the end of the survey: 'Do you have any comments?', 'Which places do you feel unsafe and why?', and 'If you could create a new space on the university campus or modify an existing space, what would it be? Why?' This article focuses on the responses to the open questions, with a particular emphasis on the open spaces.

In methodological terms, it is important to point out that we wanted to inquire about the projective dimension, that is, about the way in which those who attend the Campus daily imagine a future in material terms, the ability to design a change from the existing into something desired. However, the question 'What space in Ciudad Universitaria would you modify or create and why?' did not provide us with answers in this sense. It could be considered that the survey format in itself is not an adequate methodological tool to investigate this dimension. Since it was an important research question, we conducted in 2021 a workshop, to improve the university space, with the undergraduate seminar 'Design and Gender Studies' at the FADU-UBA[9]. In this article we show some of the projects carried out by the students.

---

9 https://dyegblog.wordpress.com/ www.instagram.com/dyeg.fadu

Idle time and pleasure on the University Campus

Figure 2: Students spend many hours in outdoor areas during the day, in spaces that are not designed for a good rest.

Photo: Authors.

In general, the open-ended responses to the survey reveal a manifest need for better design and planning of the outdoor landscape, access points and green spaces. Survey respondents would like to see upgraded walkways and lighting, along with security cameras. In other words, at a school where students learn about scales of representation and the design and reform of building structures, the conditions necessary for better inhabiting the campus is an unmet demand, as will be seen in the following section.

The survey findings reveal a set of concerns tied to practices between classes or activities. Eating, resting, smoking, talking with classmates or colleagues, and even crying: these are some of the other needs of those who study and work at FADU that take place during idle 'downtime'. Based on the open responses, these are considered quite important. Due to the characteristics of the campus, most of the university community spends this time outdoors.

In the survey, outdoor spaces were associated with gatherings and leisure during the day. Unlike the feelings of unsafety these places inspire by night, in the day, they are a source of positive affect (happiness, comfort and pleasure) for the university community (See Fig.3).

Figure 3: Outdoor esplanades. Spaces and Daily Life on the UBA Campus survey, November 2020.

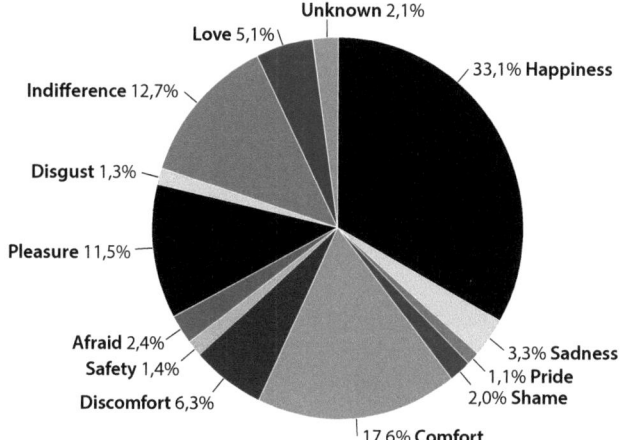

As shown in the open-ended questions, these positive affects is also accompanied by a demand for structural upgrades.

> I think the outdoor spaces could be improved. Considering that FADU is the school of architecture, it's strange that its immediate surroundings are so disconnected from student practices. There should be a space set aside for experimentation. (cisgender male student, age 20–24)

> I would add more green spaces to make the time students spend on campus more pleasant and I would redesign the parking lots: they're disgusting, a disaster. (transgender male student, age 20–24)

> I'd add a park. That would be great for the mental health of students and faculty, especially given the amount of stress everyone deals with in their day-to-day activities. (cisgender woman professor, age +33)

Beyond the value of being close to nature (The Campus is near an Ecological Reserve), the connection between outdoor spaces and rest came up frequently. During the day 'idle' space – that is, a place that can be used for purposes not related to studying or teaching – is vitally important for the university campus in general, especially considering the amount of time the community spends there. This need is also voiced in relation to building interiors:

> Another place to rest [is needed]. Many of us rest in the library – it has heat, air conditioning, and comfy sofas – but it's not really the place for relaxing

and that can distract those who come here for its original purpose. (cisgender male student, age 20–24)

There should be more 'rest' areas for cutting loose, reading or drinking mate[10] when we've got downtime. Most places on campus aren't designed for relaxing. (cisgender female student, age 20–24)

This response reveals one dimension of space that the university that in relation to its expected uses, does not respond to a "production-oriented" design a priori (Flesler, 2021). In this regard, the space most frequently mentioned is the *Siestario* (see Image 3):

I would add a large space where we can rest, wait for grades or hang out between subjects. It would be something like the *siestario* on the second floor [see Fig.4] but larger and in a well-lit, comfortable area, maybe one that is partially outdoors. (cisgender female student, age 20–24)

Some comfortable, clean place for the times when you need to spend the whole day at school, maybe after pulling an all-nighter. A place with sofas or comfy furniture for relaxing. A big *siestario*, since a lot of people would want to go. (cisgender female student, age 20–24)

In summary, this section has shown how outdoor spaces inspire different sort of demand, one for a design that facilitates relaxation and leisure. The building interiors must also be reformed, given that resting and even sleeping become necessary due to the distance between student homes and campus. As noted earlier, this means people spend many hours at the university, making downtime a significant portion of university life.

---

10 'Mate' is a very popular infusion in Argentina that has been drunk throughout the national territory for more than 200 years across social classes and generations. It is a widespread custom that is part of the national identity and is taken individually and is part of a collective ritual. It is very common to see people sharing mate at family gatherings, friends, work, and study groups. That is why it is an essential part of the university experience in the country since students meet to study, do practical work, or rest in the middle of the day and usually share mate. 'Do you want a mate?' is a question that invites you to join a conversation and share a moment with others.

Figure 4: The *siestario* ('siesta' means nap in Spanish) is an installation designed by students for reclining.

Picture: Authors.

Designing the future, materialising desires

One of the objectives of the research was also to study the projective dimension linked to the design of space, that is, the way in which those who attend the Campus daily imagine a future in material terms. In other words, the ability to design a change from the existing into something desired. For this purpose, at the end of the questionnaire we included the following question: 'If you had the possibility, what space in the Campus would you modify or create and why?' Of the 1400 total responses, 1030 people took the trouble to write, in some cases, one sentence, in others long paragraphs, and what appeared in first place is, as we observed in the previous sections, an analysis of the building conditions and demands for concrete improvements.

Therefore, the dimension of imagination linked to space was not possible to analyse in depth from the written answers received in the survey. For this reason, we decided to work in collaboration with the undergraduate seminar Design and Gender Studies at the FADU-UBA, in the realisation of a workshop in the academic period March-July 2021, in which 182 undergraduate students participated, with the aim of developing audiovisual, spatial, graphic or object design projects to improve the university space. The result was 34 projects in which students of Architecture, Industrial Design, Graphic Design, Clothing Design, Textile Design, Landscape Design and Multimedia Design participated.

For the analysis of the results obtained, the projects were grouped according to the four groups used for the survey: a) Gender spaces, b) Pedagogical spaces, c) Outdoor, meeting and transit spaces, d) Management spaces. However, once all the projects were grouped together, it was found that there was no great interest in proposing an intervention in category d, while categories b and c were the most popular, as can be seen in Figure 5 below.

Figure 5: Percentage of projects carried out by students in the following categories: a) Gender spaces, b) Pedagogical spaces, c) Outdoor, meeting and transit spaces, d) Management spaces.

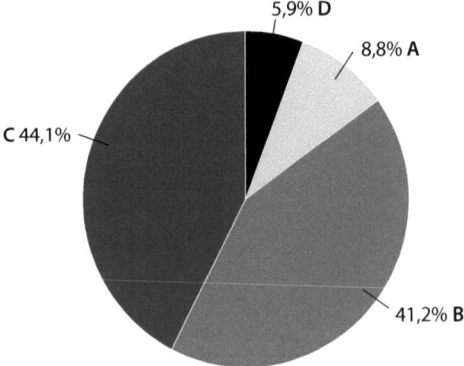

The following are some examples of projects related to the spaces discussed in this article: outdoor areas and spaces inside the building that require redesign to transform them into spaces for leisure and rest, even spaces for crying.[11]

Empantanades (In the swamp)

This project proposed to design a space for conditioning and equipment in the area of the Natural Reserve next to the Campus (colloquially called as *the swamp*). The space designed for resting allows being outdoors and sheltered. The same morphology generates floors, ceilings and seats.

---

11 To see all the projects, visit: https://dyegblog.wordpress.com/extension-y-transferencias/

Figure 6: Empantanades (In the swamp). Students: María Belén Cerviño, Delfina Halm, Daniela Alejandra Lopez Scerbo, Juliana Nastaro, Sol Ayelen Tetto.

Source: Website of the Sminar Design and Gender Studies at the FADU-UBA: https://dyegblog.wordpress.com/extension-y-transferencias/

86　Idle Uses and Body Comfort

Pulpo (Octopus)

Design of an outdoor rest and leisure area. The principal aim was to rethink the space of the School from a gender perspective, which proposes that care is not something private and individual, but social. We sought this place as an interdependence with the surroundings and the environment. It contains solar panels for heating, a hot and cold water dispenser for "mate"[12], and a plug to charge cell phones.

Figure 7: Pulpo (Octopus). Students: Camila Jazmin Acuña Fuentes, Alejandra Karina Baldovino, Leila Zubin.

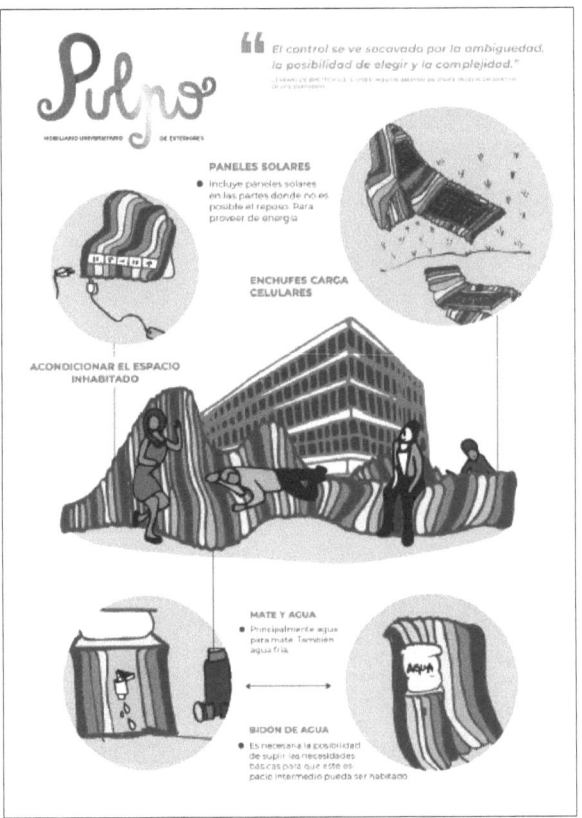

Source: Website of the Sminar Design and Gender Studies at the FADU-UBA: https://dyegblog.wordpress.com/extension-y-transferencias/

---

12 See footnote number 12.

MULTI: Mobiliario Universitario de Libre Transformación Identitaria
(University Furniture of Free Identity Transformation)

The main objective was to take over the FADU spaces most frequented by its students. In particular the corridors, usually used to wait for the delivery of notes, next to the workshops where the courses are taught. It is an equipment design that provides comfort to the diversity of corporalities that inhabit the FADU-UBA. The Mobiliario Universitario de Libre Transformación Identitaria (University Furniture of Free Identity Transformation) is made of PVC canvas and high density polyurethane foam.

Figure 8: MULTI: Mobiliario Universitario de Libre Transformación Identitaria (University Furniture of Free Identity Transformation). Students: Candela Paula Aris, Lucas Hernán Casavalle, Carolina Hobert, Carolina Fernández, Julieta Schierenbeck, Federico Villalba.

Source: Website of the Sminar Design and Gender Studies at the FADU-UBA: https://dyegblog.wordpress.com/extension-y-transferencias/

La llorería: Un lugar para llorar. (A place for crying)[13]

Given the lack of leisure spaces for those students who usually spend a lot of time at FADU, and who at the same time report feeling overwhelmed by both the number of courses and the time load. La Llorería is a space designed for leisure, relaxation and crying.

Figure 9: La llorería: Un lugar para llorar. (A place for crying) ('Llorar' in Spanish is cry). Students: Aldana Casais, Valentina Morales, Daniela Obella, Mariana Ferreira.

Spataro y Flesler

The projects in general show a very high level of place attachment and appropriation of the university space. According to Tomeu Vidal Moranta and Enric Pol Urrútia (2005) there is a dual model of appropriation or place attachment: action-transformation and symbolic identification. While the former is linked to the idea of territoriality, symbolic identification is linked to affective processes. 'Through action on the environment, individuals, groups and collectivities transform space, leaving their 'footprint' in it, that is, symbolically charged signs and marks. Through action, the person incorporates the environment into his or her

---

13 'Llorar' in Spanish is cry.

cognitive and affective processes in an active and updated manner.' (Moranta 2005: 283). In this sense we read the projects designed by students about their university space. Their feeling of appropriation allowed us to detect a multiplicity of problems regarding the materiality and daily living in the Campus and, in particular, the need to have spaces for leisure and rest, in continuity with what we analysed from the data collected in the survey.

For the category of Outdoor Spaces, meeting and transit spaces, a problem that arises is the lack of planning and furniture in indoor spaces that are not considered 'pedagogical', such as corridors, central courtyard, stairs. Questions arise such as 'Who didn't eat sitting on the floor, in some corner?'; 'Which student did not take a nap somewhere in the pavilion?' 'How long did you wait for a note in the corridor?'. Likewise, with respect to outdoor spaces, there is a manifest need to generate places for leisure and sociability outside the pedagogical or management spaces. This coincides with the results of the survey where outdoor spaces, meeting and leisure spaces, such as the Siestario, are among the most positively evaluated by the university community.

In summary, we consider it fundamental in the last stage of the research to add the voice of the students (as native subjects of the university spatiality) in the design of projects informed by the intersection between Design and Gender Studies. Their proposals resulted in the materialisation of many of the findings obtained from the survey. It also allowed us to approach and explore the affective dimension and the attachment to the place at a time when they were forced not to inhabit that space. Affective memory operated as one more element when projecting and added commitment to the projects.

Conclusions

> I think the outdoor spaces could be improved. Considering that FADU is the school of architecture, it's strange that its immediate surroundings are so disconnected from student practices. There should be a space set aside for experimentation. (cisgender male professor, age 33+)

The goal of this article was to analyse the connections between affect, gender and space on a University of Buenos Aires campus in the context of recent transformations in the gender agenda at Argentine universities. Specifically, the article focused on analysing what spaces were important to this community and what proposals for changes were most common. The combination of a campus far removed from the centre of the city, a school focused on the study of design, and the launch of gender policies at this same school made FADU a logical site to explore the questions posed as part of this research.

The open-ended questions from the survey enabled a more in-depth look at the emotions most frequently cited in the quantitative answers. Student stories reveal that beyond the university's size, prestige and history as a tuition-free institution accessible to all, other factors come into play when reflecting on the university experience.

One novel and unforeseen finding of the study was the great demand for facilities both outdoors and indoors designed for downtime, relaxation and leisure. As underscored by the survey, taking and giving classes are only part of inhabiting FADU and what happens between these activities is meaningful for its community. As noted in the quote from the professor above, at a school dedicated to the study of design, the lack of policies in which design becomes an instrument for wellbeing is particularly paradoxical.

References

Ahmed, S. (2004): *The Cultural Politics of Emotion*, Edinburgh: Edinburgh University Press.
Ahmed, S. (2010): *The Promise of Happiness*, Durham: Duke University Press.
Azparren, A., Oberti, A./ Spataro, C. (2022): *Reconocer para transformar: primeros diagnósticos sobre situaciones de violencia de género en la Universidad de Buenos Aires.* Sociales en Debate No. 15. Facultad de Ciencias Sociales-UBA.
Barrancos, D. (2007): *Mujeres en la sociedad argentina. Una historia de cinco siglos,* Buenos Aires: Sudamericana.
Berlant, L. (2011): *Cruel Optimism.* Durham: Duke University Press.
Blanco, R./ Flesler, G./ Spataro, C. (2021): Superficies de placer, orgullo y asco. Afectos y géneros en la espacialidad del campus universitario. Revista Academia XXII, *12 (24)*, 135–158.
Carli, S. (Ed.) (2022): *Historia de la Universidad de Buenos Aires. Tomo III (1945–1983).* Eudeba.
CPAU (2011). Moderna Buenos Aires. https://www.modernabuenosaires.org/obras/20s-a-70s/ciudad-universitaria-uba---pabellones-2-y-3.
Davison, J./Bondi, L./Smith, M. (Eds.) (2006): *Emotional Geographies.* London: Routledge.
Flesler, G. (2021): El espacio universitario generizado: apropiaciones y desvíos. In A. Buzaglo (Ed.): *Feminismos, Arquitecturas y Territorios.* A&P Ediciones Especiales, *44.* Universidad Nacional de Rosario.
Flesler, G./Thus, V. (2022): Experiencias de igualdad en la Universidad de Buenos Aires. In G. Bonder (Ed.) *La institucionalización del enfoque de igualdad de género en universidades de América Latina: experiencias, reflexiones y contribuciones para el futuro de la educación superior* (151–165). Flacso.

Flesler, G./Martin, A. L./Quaglino, A./Spataro, C. (2020): Buenas compañeras: genealogía de un modo de trabajo colaborativo y feminista en la universidad. In: D. Losiggio & M. Solana (Eds.) *Acciones y debates feministas en las universidades* (85-112). Editorial UNAJ.

Hooks, B. (1994): *Teaching to Transgress: Education as the Practice of Freedom.* New York, NY: Routledge.

Vidal Moranta, T./Pol Urrútia, E. (2005): La apropiación del espacio: una propuesta teórica para comprender la vinculación entre las personas y los lugares. Anuario de Psicología, vol. 36, nº 3, Universitat de Barcelona, 281–297.

Zaragocin, S./ Caretta. M. A. (2021): 'Cuerpo-Territorio: A Decolonial Feminist Geographical Method for the Study of Embodiment', *Annals of the American Association of Geographers*, 111(5): 1503-1518. https://doi.org/10.1080/24694452.2020.1812370

Involve and Intervene

Julia Pierzina

The current crisis evolving around climate, war, the search for belonging, fights for justice, visibility and distribution, are a call to action and ask us as designers to get involved. I call on us to be vigilant in designing in a crisis-appropriate and sustainable way – even to design in a way that supports resilience not the market. If we want to know how justice materialises, if we want to know how fairness materialises, we have to ask questions:

Who participates? Who does not? Why not? Who benefits? Whose benefits are limited and why? What barriers exist? Which paths are usable for whom? Who needs support? What kind of support?

As designers, we can no longer afford to view resources as endless. We cannot afford to make decisions based on aesthetics that serve the market and in turn support the recognition of our own professional activity. I advocate accepting the tasks that impose themselves on us – reductions that stand for social coexistence, resource conservation, equity and fairness. This can be in schools and at cemeteries, at bus stops and in queues, at the counter and in emergency situations. We can dare and allow ourselves to break out of our categories of design directions and become aware of the social dimensions of all our design decisions. Design shows how fairness, justice, access, hierarchies, discrimination and exploitation materialise. Because of that, those who are involved in the development of the artifacts must take responsibility.

Design exacerbates and even creates social injustices and confirms systems that divide people into classes based on various characteristics and/or attributions. Who benefits when we use the trivialisation of 'defensive design' to make design decisions that exclude people and make their lives more difficult? Park benches on which it is impossible to lie down, highly frequented permanent sounds in front of 'prestigious buildings' or pop-up flower pots in places that were previously sought out as protective niches by people without shelter – numerous examples can be observed where designers have deliberately come up with interventions to make life difficult for people. And not all people, but especially those who are themselves restricted in their freedom of design – e.g. people living on the street. Maria Cecilia Loschiavo dos Santos has collected numerous examples of this from major cities and documented them photographically. We have an astonishingly large number of terms to describe design decisions in public space that exacerbate discrimination (hostile architecture, defensive architecture, hostile design, deterrent design, defensive urban design, unpleasant design, exclusionary design ...). Design according to gender data gaps leads to gender based disadvantages and injustices. Drugs that have not been tested on women, intelligent software that has not been trained with gender-specific data. There are more and more examples of how we use design decisions to make hierarchies and thus also disadvantages an instrument, an amplifier. This cannot be accepted!

But where to start? How to intervene? The Sustainable Development Goals make it easy for us and also provide us a designers' task list that we have to work through. Every day, again and again and with all our roles, we can visualise the goals and achieve them with our own skills. Not only as designers, but also as fellow citizens, as neighbours, as consumers.

After an intensive examination of discrimination structures and othering processes in the field of migration and immigration history, I focused my own design practice on the identification of gender inequities in adolescence. Choosing the field of school as a research context was met with a lot of resistance and rejection. Intervening means interfering – and that can sometimes be unpleasant:

Interfere and intervene

In 'IUI Propädeutik der Intervention', Friedrich von Borries and Mara Recklies write about an 'interventionist desire' (Borries/Recklies 2017: 37) as a description of design motivation. I am enthusiastic about this perspective and would like to share it as an appeal and thus motivate a liberation from narrow perspectives on exclusive design spaces, towards opening up to new interfaces and taking responsibility as designers. To show what this is all about, we need to understand the sphere of influence – the intervention – as a situation. According to Friedrich von Borries and Mara Recklies, an intervention is 'an action that does not refer to itself, but is defined as a relational practice by reference to the existing' (Borries/Recklies 2017: 14). In the design process, this means that design only happens when it interacts with the surrounding entities – whether human, natural or artificial. The interaction with an artifact therefore also determines a property of the artifact that was already intended or at least considered by the designer in advance. Non-handling, which would rather be non-use, also provides information about the artifact. Its impracticality describes something about the creation process. Which perspectives were neglected, which characteristics prevent users from interacting with the artifact? If we, as designers, enter into observation with the perspective of the designable, experience it and can contribute new designs, adaptations and changes through our filters, experiences and perspectives, then we can use this interventionist desire as a common dynamic. When Griselda Flesler (Flesler 2023:27) speaks of 'smuggling feminism into androcentric institution' (Place 2023: 24-27), she is referring to tasks and responsibilities for social processes in design theory and in the development of artifacts. She includes feminist methods in her teaching and observes a growing interest on the part of design students in dealing with social challenges and demands. I also like to take up the concept of 'smuggling' and would like to encourage designers to 'smuggle' themselves into areas that have not been classified as relevant to design yet. 'The [...] term that I have used is to smuggle, which has to do with material or symbolic actions that challenge and crack the borders'(Flesler 2023: 27).

Just as we have to deal with the dissolution of clear 'areas of responsibility' in any design discipline, we can also endure the fact that the act of an intervention marks an intermediate situation in the design process – the intervention describes 'an existence between clear assignments and classifications' (Borries/Recklies 2017: 15). Especially in our ambiguity-intolerant society, this is precisely what is difficult to endure.

Clarifying the possible relationship between *research and design* helps us to open up new fields of activity and to assert ourselves in them. We currently differentiate between three categories: research on/about design, research for design and research by/through design. *Research on/about design* means researching an artefact – i.e. describing and analysing its history, components, use, etc. *Research for design* describes a two-phase principle that is causally related. First, research is carried out in order to then deal with it further in design. I would see this transition from research into a design process as interdisciplinary work. For me, the most fascinating relationship between research and design is *research by/through design*. Here, research and design are so interwoven that a clear separation is hardly possible. Methods from other disciplines are taken up and combined or modelled with design-methodological approaches. It is interesting to note here that design decisions are also made in research work in disciplines other than design. Starting with the development of a research question, the research interest, the inclusion of data sources and authors, and the sampling. I consider all these curatorial decisions to be design decisions, as they are decisive in shaping the revelations/ (it is not for nothing that we also speak of 'research design' in disciplines other than design). In addition, *research by/through design* also describes the interventionist character of designers in their fields of research. Their own presence during participant observation alone shapes and frames the insights gained. The confrontation with artifacts also provides information about the research subjects. In the social sciences, visual and audio materials are often used to collect data. Starting with the settings of interview situations, existing objects, media material and metaphors to the selection of the spatial environment (space, presence, sounds, context) have an influence on the data collected. Finally, *research by/through design* can also be '[p]raxis-led design research, [...] which [...] in this sense does not simply want to explore practice with scientific methods but generates new knowledge with the means and procedures of design practice itself' (Mareis 2014: 185). These (design) qualities can be utilized. Particularly when investigating the 'use and reception of design artifacts' (ibid.: 102), design is understood both as a *survey method and as an evaluation perspective*. Following this road I intervene in fields that have not yet been declared a 'design field'. By combining different methods, research through design makes it possible to investigate 'complex[...] dynamics that unfold between tradition, socially anchored convention and its break, between intention and serendipity, between conscious and implicit forms of action' (ibid.: 24). This kind of transdisciplinarity is suitable because social structures are characterised by power and hierarchy. Categories such as gender, age, capability and restraint, language, appearance and level of education must be investigated using various tools and methods across and between disciplines, because 'contextually novel combinations of existing knowledge and particular research findings [are necessary in order to] create or bring about something new' (Schneider 2005: 274). With 'socially oriented design research' (Borries/Fezer 2013: 75), we have the opportunity to observe and analyse social structures in order to then expose them to interventions in a second step. Interventions are then transformation processes that '[tear] openings in the incrustations of the existing [and] create situations that can be the starting point for something new' (Borries/Recklies 2017: 32f.). For as we know, and as the design theorist and design philosopher Julia-Constance Dissel has already formulated, 'design structures, shapes and changes the lifeworld through its symbolic and its physically tangible facticity and resistance, and with it, people themselves' (Dissel 2016: 14).

Social justice is not just about checking for advantages and disadvantages. Lived and reproduced norms all too often dismantle rights. For example, gender-specific attributions have a much greater impact on the reality of young people's lives than the law of equality that is enshrined in the German constitution. Through repetition, imitation and a lack of questioning, the so-called gender scripts are an essential part of young people's idea of norms, which means that actual gender equity is still a long way off. I was able to gather these insights during my research work as a designer in the research field of 'Gender Design & School'.

When trying to acquire a school for my field research, administrations and all school-organising authorities thought of me as an outsider and referred me to school psychology or social pedagogy as they had 'something to do with gender'. Those who deal with social grievances are social pedagogues and psychologists – those who are concerned are then people who deviate from a social norm. This attitude made it significantly more difficult to 'get involved in new fields of action' at the beginning of the research. At the same time, these stereotypes show that it is important to assert oneself as a designer and to shake up fields and responsibilities – simply in order to gain new insights.

But what does it mean to get involved in order to do something good? What can give us a guideline and what starting points do we choose? Mara Recklies has drawn up a criteriology of design and asks in her article about the criteria for good design. Her observation is that the claim to achieve 'good design' usually involves three aspects of 'good' – good in the sense of aesthetic/stylish, good in the sense of functional and good in the sense of human-centred. She describes in detail that many developments that could be labelled as 'good' thanks to at least one of these categories do not adhere to today's contemporary standards of 'good'. The question of functionality is also always about who the target group of the functionality is, what happens to the non-expected target groups in interaction with the artifact and also what other consequences are inherent in functionalism from the manufacturing process to disposal (Recklies in Rodatz/Smolarski 2021:102ff.). In her article, she also criticises the fact that the third legitimisation of 'good' – the label 'human-centered design' – is often only associated as modern and progressive and is not actually human-centered. Often, it is not 'the human' that is used as a benchmark for development, but, as Caroline Criado Perez explains in her book 'Invisible Women' in many ways, the 'average man', white, middle-aged in the global West (Perez 2020). What Perez shows emphatically, and Mara Recklies underlines in her contribution is that the diversity of people does not permeate even the claim of 'human-centredness' and that design processes are still too often targeted at a certain group that only makes up a fraction of the population. So, how do we do something good with design then and deal with the crisis of the world and empower ourselves to open up new fields of design? Before an artifact is 'finished', it should be ensured that no one suffers or is harmed by, with, through or even because of the artifact and the interaction in social environments. An adequate means of mitigating the dangers in the design process described here is critical self-examination in design decisions and concrete collaboration with end users and perhaps especially those who are not expected to use/implement/experience the artifact. If good design is oriented towards the needs, interests and usage scenarios of the users (Bieling 2020: 62), then the needs, interests and everyday practices must be deeply researched and deconstructed. I will outline one way of doing this below by explaining my idea of inverse artefact analysis.

Making it inversive

One method from research on design is called 'artifact analysis' (Lueger/Froschauer 2018). Here, a specific artifact is deconstructed and analysed in terms of its components in order to gain insights into it. This view of the artifact is well established. Joachim Kobuss proposes the distinction of non-haptic artifacts into mentefacts and sociofacts. He thus separates mentefacts as 'mental design by means of consultation' and sociofacts as 'design of social relationships in processes' (Kobuss 2022; 10, 23). This attempt at separation is based on the new accounting services provided by designers to differentiate their work. The concept of separation is very exciting but runs into difficulties the first time it is conjugated. In social interaction, where are the boundaries between what is purely thought, behaviour adapted to social expectations and expressions?

According to the current state of research, I follow the concept of socio-design formulated by Bazon Brock that takes up the idea that artifacts are to be understood in the non-material sense as 'control principles' or 'abstract, non-objective organisational principles' (Borries/Fezer 2013: 79). But how do we get from a normal artifact analysis, where we look at what is there and reduce it to its state in an isolated way and describe it, to here? What about the social sphere surrounding the artifact, the interaction, the use, the establishment, possible avoidance? What if we even look at the wrong artifact sphere to handle a specific problem like gender imbalance, for example? Here comes my idea of a different form of artifact analysis. Lueger and Froschauer explain: "[t]o understand artifacts, one must consider the social world behind them; and to understand the social world, one must consider the artifacts handled in it" (Lueger/Froschauer 2018: 7). I propose a principle that only reveals the artifact at the end of the analysis. The *'inverse artefact analysis'* carries out an in-depth analysis *in the field of social entanglement* through observation and interventions in order to finally enable identification of relevant artifacts or artiact areas for making situations better, fairer, more sustainable. This contrasts our established version of artifact analysis in design. Especially in social contexts with disadvantages, discrimination and hierarchies involved, inverse artifact analysis is about recognising existing structures and understanding structures and patterns by intervening from within in order to question and criticise these patterns. For an 'intervention designer', the design process in social interactions first lies in the visualization of attributions and carriers of meaning. Simplifications and hasty decisions to categorise reinforce disadvantages, demarcation and hierarchies. In order to discover these social grievances as a field of action, the subliminal, successive and tenacious everyday practices must be identified in the field and then made discussable for designing. So, we use the theory of symbolic interactionism, asserting *inverse artefact analysis* as a means of capturing levels of interaction and meaning carriers, and then using design decisions to plan interventions. Researching people as phenomena in relation to their material and immaterial environment '[...] is the task of design science in order to create offers that include people and not exclude them' (Foraita in Bieling 2020: 63).

Into the field

In order to outline the depth and complexity of social interactions, to make them workable and also designable, I will provide an insight into my own design theory and social science research below. In order to describe the 'materialisation of fairness', we must therefore also recognise the 'materialisation of unfairness'. In my research, the focus was on perceived gender equity in the context of a school – this also included finding out how images of gender and gender affiliation are formed, how they are applied in everyday school life and also how students deal with irritations in the already established – also gendered – norms. In order to answer these questions, 'moments of routine and internalised experiential knowledge' (Mareis 2014: 188) must be made visible. Consistent triangulation (Flick et al. 2008: 309f.) based on grounded theory methodology should provide a remedy. Iterative data collection with different formats enabled the concretisation of questions and the development of key topics that were placed by the researched group.

In order to answer the research question according to the principles of grounded theory, the principles of openness, processuality and communication guided the approach. The research question was: '*Which artifacts determine the gender perceptions of pupils aged 14 to 16 in the context of the school*?'. The following survey methods were selected to answer the questions: participant observation, qualitative individual interviews, group discussions.

I will now briefly discuss the special qualities of these methods from a design perspective and thus call for imitation: Participant observation means actually moving into the field you want to explore. The aim here is to create a path into everyday routines through gatekeepers. This is done by the 'observed' accepting an observing person and normalising this observation in such a way that it can be assumed that the behaviour does not differ significantly from behaviour that would have occurred without the presence of a researcher. This acceptance in the field can be achieved through a lot of patience, the correct introduction (role) in the field and consistency in the observation. It is also important here that the researcher accepts that they do not have a 'neutral view' of the observed situation. Every selected sequence, every decision as to where attention is directed, already frames the data basis and thus also the basis for later interpretation of the data. In my case, after several attempts to make contact with different schools, I met with tutors from one class to discuss the role I would take on in everyday school life in the selected class (the sampling). The tutors were thus gatekeepers in an otherwise rather closed social space, such as a class community.

Over several months, I spent an average of three days a week in a school class, experienced their everyday routines, had conversations with them and witnessed situations that were perceived as disruptive. These provided high-quality examples for the individual discussions that were planned later. In particular, 'in-between moments' in break scenarios or in waiting situations provided deep insights into the negotiation processes between the pupils. During these observations of routines, conflicts, everyday practices and confrontations, I regularly noted observations, transcribed dialogs between pupils and drew spatial scenarios for documentation. These notes helped enormously in reconstructing references for the individual interviews. They also provided initial directions for clustering.

In addition to the more passively oriented role of an observer, planned interventions in everyday school life served as an initial check of the aspects I had previously identified. In order to approach the research with a concrete question, the interactions, which could be games, surveys or scenario developments, for example, provided relevant topics for the pupils. Of course, the role of the researcher in the room remains a special feature. Even when I was introduced as a trainee, not all of the teachers teaching the class group were at the same level of information or had the same attitude. Their way of interacting with me diluted the role of an observer to a participant in the lesson. For example, I was asked to participate in foreign language lessons and was called upon to answer questions in a way that is only reserved for pupils. This kind of role confusion/role irritation could be absorbed to the extent that I was present in pupils' day-to-day life at school for such a long period of time that we could also talk about my roles in one-on-one conversations, e.g. in the playground, and the pupils could ask any questions they were interested in.

After this lengthy preparation in the participatory field observation with notes and interventions, a relationship of trust had already been established, which provided for the individual interviews in the next step of the research design. The individual interviews are also a special challenge and opportunity for the participating pupils. Some of the students agreed to an individual interview because they were happy to 'finally be able to talk about it'. What they wanted to talk about was very different. The task of a semi-structured interview is then, based on the research question, to ask the interviewee about their attitudes, values without being restrictive in advance. A key feature of the grounded theory methodology is to guarantee openness and processuality, so that pupils were able to set their own relevance in the interviews and thus also lead the conversation at times. This 'luxury' of digression opened up completely new perspectives and approaches to understanding gender constructions in everyday school life. The interviews took place in familiar settings for the young people and were introduced with small, playful questions. For post-processing, they were recorded acoustically with the written consent of the pupils and their parents or their legal guardians. A semi-structured interview consists of various blocks of questions – introductory questions, sensitisation questions, narrative-generating questions, confrontation questions [in which an active reaction/counter-reaction is required] and open questions ['Do you want to add anything else, or is there something you find important here that we haven't talked about yet?']. Depending on the sampling and the question, this list of questions should be well prepared and checked for leading questions. Particularly concise findings could be derived from the images used by pupils, especially regarding the distribution of roles and tasks in the pupils' immediate social environment.

After the individual interviews were completed, the group discussion method was used. The format, which is predestined for researching negotiation processes live and very closely, is included as a kind of 'control group' in the iterative research method of this triangulation. People who were reluctant to be interviewed individually agreed to talk to the group in a protected setting. At the beginning, a visual stimulus was introduced to trigger the group thematically in a playful way. In this case, the stimulus was a comic excerpt about partner relationships, jealousy and self-expression. Pupils read the comic together and reacted spontaneously and directly. These reactions were then the starting point for a long discussion among pupils. If a topic was deemed to be exhausted, I used brief impulses to introduce new suggestions for discussion, which were accepted or redirected, thus expanding the field for future interviews and setting the tone. The group discussions confirmed some of the indications from the participant observation and could also be used in part as a corrective – situations experienced together were renegotiated as a reference in the group discussion and the multiple perspectives provided a dynamic for renegotiating one's own attitudes. The proximity to the research of Judith Conrads supported initial findings in my work with regard to tolerance of ambiguity, demarcation and also perspectives of concern. After processing all of the collected data, structuring, coding and clustering, core categories emerged that significantly guided the naming of artifacts. The use of methods from the social sciences, interlinked with design theories on artifacts and intervention, ultimately resulted in the development of four explicit artifact clusters concerning young people's gender perceptions at school: Language and knowledge + social correctness; Mimesis and different treatment by teachers; Groups, recognition and power; Binarity, clothing and appearance and 'The world is not made for me'. My analyses of the artifacts show one striking feature: young people's ideas about gender are never directly based on products and materials, but almost exclusively on social interactions between people. Their own experiences, adventures and also knowledge as immaterial artifacts are thus the starting point for new design processes. My study also reveals that (1) young people already have initial knowledge of gender diversity beyond a binary heterosexual gender order; (2) young people often postulate that 'equality for all' is a fundamental right; (3) young people proclaim individualism: 'Everyone can be who they want to be', and also use this as an invitation to others. The greatest danger that can be identified in the idea of gender among young people relates to the constantly repeated proclamation of equality. The young people seem to be blinded by their own statements, so that they develop misperceptions of injustice and ultimately ignore them. Although they do feel injustice at times, they find it difficult to articulate it and to demand change.

The challenge for designers derived from the identified artifacts is now to respond to the immaterial artifacts with interventions. As the analysis showed in detail, the ability to change a situation depends heavily on the expressiveness of all actors – teachers, students and other people involved in the social space of the school.[1]

The lesson I can draw from this is that transdisciplinary research can uncover insights that would otherwise be denied to us. It also means that as designers, we can pay attention to life situations that we shape multidimensionally – i.e. in

---

[1] For further background information see Pierzina (2025).

different roles. In particular, sensitive, fragile, delicate life circumstances, situations or moments of discrimination can be revealed through a strong *inverse artefact analysis* and thus made workable. I see Bitten Stetter's work on dying (finally.), Tanja Godlewsky's work on death (Digitaler Todomat) and the work of Juliane Kühr (vruit) and Anastasia Kalensky (sex and pleasureable) as inspiration. In addition, numerous in-between spaces present themselves to us as design spaces: the retirement home, language in public space, waiting situations, homelessness and shelter constructions, cemetery scenarios and so on. The power of scripts is huge – both in terms of gender and other social categories. An idea of 'correct' behaviour promotes conformity, compliance and the search for fit. This shows that the most difficult form of 'materialisation of fairness' is 'non-materialisation'. It is indirect, ambiguous and therefore vulnerable. The nuances and nuances are difficult to understand and therefore difficult to address. The methods presented here – from field observation to the superstructure of 'inverse artefact analysis' are intended to help discover subliminal nuances, describe them and then be able to process them.

References

Bieling, T. (2020). Gender (&) Design: Positionen zur Vergeschlechtlichung in Gestaltungskulturen (Design Meanings, Band 2). Sesto S. Giovanni: Mimesis International.

Borries, F. v./Recklies, M. (2017). IUI Propädeutik der Intervention. Leipzig: Merve Verlag.

Borries, F.v. /Fezer, J. (2013). Weil Design die Welt verändert... Texte zur Gestaltung. Gestalten – ein Projekt der HFBK Hamburg.

Brandes, U./Erlhoff, M./ Schemmann, N. (2009). Designtheorie und Designforschung. Stuttgart: Wilhelm Fink GmbH & Co. Verlags-KG.

Criado-Perez, C. (2020). Unsichtbare Frauen. Wie eine von Männern gemachte Welt die Hälfte der Bevölkerung ignoriert. München: btb Verlag.

Denzin, N. K. (N.N.). Symbolischer Interaktionismus. In: Flick, U./ Von Kardorff, E. /Steinke, I. (Eds.) (2008). Qualitative Forschung: Ein Handbuch (6.Auflage). Berlin: Rowohlt Taschenbuch Verlag.

Dissel, J.-C. (Ed.) (2016). Design & Philosophie. Schnittstellen und Wahlverwandtschaften. Bielefeld: transcript Verlag.

Flesler, G. (2023). On smuggling feminism into design institutions. In: Place, Alison. (2023). Feminist Designer. On the Personal and the Political in Design. Cambridge: The MIT Press, 23-27.

Flick, U./ Von Kardorff, E./Steinke, I. (Eds.) (2008). Qualitative Forschung: Ein Handbuch (6.Auflage). Berlin: Rowohlt Taschenbuch Verlag.

Foraita, S. (N.N.) Gender studies und Designwissenschaften. In: Bieling, T. (2020). Gender (&) Design: Positionen zur Vergeschlechtlichung in Gestaltungskulturen (Design Meanings, Band 2). Sesto S. Giovanni: Mimesis International, 57-64.
Kobuss, J. (2022): Studie zur wirtschaftlichen Relevanz von Design. Bayern design GmbH.
Krippendorff, K. (2013). Die semantische Wende. Eine neue Grundlage für Design. Schriften zur Gestaltung. Basel: Birkhäuser Verlag.
Kubandt, M. (2017): Zur Rolle als Geschlechterforscherin im frühpädagogischen Feld zwischen Subjektivität, (Re-)Konstruktion und Reifikation. In: Stenger, U./Edelmann, D./ Nolte, D./Schulz, M. (Eds.): Diversität in der Pädagogik der frühen Kindheit. Weinheim: Beltz Juventa, 271-285.
Kubandt, M. (2016). Geschlechterdifferenzierung in der Kindertageseinrichtung: Eine qualitativ-rekonstruktive Studie (Studien zu Differenz, Bildung und Kultur). Opladen; Berlin; Toronto: Verlag Barbara Budrich.
Lueger, M./Froschauer, U. (2018): Artefaktanalyse: Grundlagen und Verfahren (Qualitative Sozialforschung). Wiesbaden: Springer VS.
Mareis, C. (2014). Theorien des Designs. Zur Einführung. Hamburg: Junius Verlag.
Mareis, C./Held, M./Joost, G. (Eds.) (2013). Wer gestaltet die Gestaltung Praxis, Theorie und Geschichte des partizipatorischen Designs. Bielefeld: transcript Verlag.
Milev, Y. (ed.) (2013) Design Kulturen. Der erweiterte Designbegriff im Entwurfsfeld der Kulturwissenschaften. HfG Forschung (5. Edition). Paderborn: Brill | Fink.
Pierzina, J. (2025). Gender Design Schule. Bielefeld: transcript Verlag.
Place, A. (2023). Feminist Designer. On the Personal and the Political in Design. Cambridge; Massachusetts, London: The MIT Press.
Rech, S. (2006). Wie eine andere Welt. Eine Grounded Theory-Studie zur Frage der Teilhabe von Eltern an schulischer Kommunikation am Beispiel von RealschülerInnen. Mainz: Johannes Gutenberg-Universität http://doi.org/10.25358/openscience-4156.
Recklies, M. (2021). Kriterien für gutes Design, die den Schaden maximieren. Zur Kriteriologie der Gestaltung. In: Rodatz, C./Smolarski, P. (2021): Wie können wir den Schaden maximieren? Gestaltung trotz Komplexität. Beiträge zu einem Public Interest Design (1. Edition). Bielefeld: transcript Verlag.
Rodatz, C./Smolarski, P. (2021). Wie können wir den Schaden maximieren?: Gestaltung trotz Komplexität. Beiträge zu einem Public Interest Design (1. Edition). Bielefeld: transcript Verlag.
Schneider, B. (2005). Design – eine Einführung. Entwurf im sozialen, kulturellen und wirtschaftlichen Kontext. Basel; Boston; Berlin: Birkhäuser Verlag.
Schweppenhäuser, G. (2003). Grundbegriffe der Ethik. Zur Einführung. Hamburg: Junius Verlag.

Glossary

Petromasculinity

Academics have used the concept of petromasculinity to critique how the environmental impacts of the fossil fuel industry are often downplayed or ignored in favour of preserving notions of masculine power and control over natural resources. It suggests that masculinity, in this context, is entangled with environmental destruction and economic systems that rely on the continued exploitation of natural resources. The term petromasculinity is therefore used to critique the current power structures at play and the economic systems that seem to rely on petrochemicals and energy extraction, which very often is at odds with sustainability and environmental goals.

Gender Fairness & Gender Equality

Gender Equality refers to a state in which individuals, regardless of their gender, have equal rights, opportunities, and access to resources. It focuses on the idea that all genders should have the same social, economic, and political rights and that there should be no legal or systemic discrimination based on gender. Gender equality often involves policies and actions that aim to eliminate discrimination by creating for example equal pay for equal work, the right to vote, and access to education for those that are restricted in their rights.

Gender Fairness, on the other hand, goes deeper and emphasizes the necessity to also recognise the different needs and contextual circumstances of individuals based on their gender. It is not just about treating everyone the same but ensuring that everyone gets what they need to succeed. This may involve implementing policies or practices that account for unequal starting points due to gender-based discrimination or societal expectations. For example, gender fairness might involve offering special support to women in male-dominated fields or ensuring that men have opportunities to take parental leave, which might not be traditionally available to them.

Ecofeminism

Ecofeminism is an interdisciplinary theory and social movement that combines ecological and feminist perspectives. It postulates that the exploitation of nature and the oppression of women and other marginalized groups are closely linked and reinforced by patriarchal structures and capitalist economic systems. Ecofeminists argue that dominance over nature and the oppression of women are not isolated phenomena, but rather expressions of a shared system of domination and control. They emphasize that the power relations that affect both the environment and social gender relations are in a complex, reciprocal relationship with each other. Ecofeminism argues for an equal, sustainable and solidary society that respects both human rights including everyone and the ecological integrity of the earth.

Design Scripts

Design scripts in relation to gender are theoretical and methodological concepts that address the ways in which design practices and processes influence and shape gender roles and identities. The term describes the implicit, culturally and socially shaped norms, values, assumptions and structures that are integrated into any design process and that guide the way products, technologies and systems are designed. In terms of gender design scripts refer to how design practices unconsciously or intentionally reproduce or challenge certain gender dichotomies and stereotypes (e.g. masculinity and femininity). Design scripts can be manifested in the functional aspects of products as well as in their aesthetic or symbolic dimensions by defining certain expectations of users' behaviour and needs based on their gender.

Intersectionality & Intersectional Design

Intersectionality is a concept that explores how different aspects of a person's identity—such as gender, race, class, sexuality, ability, religion, and other social factors—interact and overlap to create unique systems of privilege or oppression. The term was first coined by Kimberlé Crenshaw to describe how Black women, in particular, experience discrimination in ways that cannot be understood by looking at race or gender separately, but must be understood as interconnected.

Intersectional design is an approach to designing products, services, experiences, or systems that considers the diverse and overlapping identities and needs of individuals, recognizing how factors such as race, gender, class, ability, age, sexuality, and more interact and influence people's experiences. It applies the principles of intersectionality to the design process, ensuring that the solutions created are inclusive and accessible to a wide variety of people with diverse social identities and backgrounds. Intersectional design moves beyond inclusive design as it is not only directed toward the needs of specific marginalised groups which need to be included, but also focuses on the interwoven nature of different claims arising from diverse categories of discrimination. Intersectional design addresses power dynamics since it seeks to recognise and dismantle power structures that might be the source of exclusions. It considers how power, privilege, and oppression play a role in shaping experiences and tries to create design solutions that challenge and disrupt those inequalities.

Gender Gaps

Gender Pay Gap

The gender pay gap refers to the difference in average earnings between women and men in the workforce. It is typically expressed as a percentage, representing how much less women earn compared to men, on average, for similar work or across different sectors. The gender pay gap can be measured in different ways: The Unadjusted Pay Gap is the most common measure and looks at the average income of all men and women, regardless of job type, experience, or hours worked. This measure shows the overall difference in earnings between the sexes, which includes all contributing factors, including discrimination, career choices, and family responsibilities. The Adjusted Pay Gap takes into account factors like occupation, hours worked, education, and experience. It focuses on the difference in pay for men and women who are in similar roles or have similar qualifications. This gap is usually narrower than the unadjusted pay gap but still reflects inequalities that might stem from unconscious bias and workplace discrimination.

Gender Tech Gap

The gender tech gap refers to the disparity between men and women in terms of access to, participation in, and representation within the technology sector. This gap can manifest in various ways, including unequal representation in tech jobs, unequal access to technology, and differences in how technology is developed and used by different genders. The gender tech gap is particularly strong in areas like software development, engineering, AI, and leadership roles within tech companies, where women and gender minorities are still underrepresented. According to various reports, women currently only make up around 27,6 % of the global tech workforce. It also encompasses issues related to the design and development of technology, where gender biases shape the products and services created, resulting in technology that does not fully meet the needs of all users. Many tech products and platforms are developed with a predominantly male perspective, which can lead to gender biases in the design of algorithms, software, and hardware. For example, voice assistants like Siri or Alexa have historically been designed with default female voices, reinforcing the stereotype of the female as submissive service person. To close the tech gap we need to encourage girls in STEM fields, inspiring them to pursue tech education, such as coding, we need more inclusive hiring practices and structures, advocating for more women in leadership roles and last but not least we need to address gender biases in general, and create awareness for example through creation of diverse design teams and auditing algorithms for biases.

Index

Artifact Analysis

Capitalism
Care
Communication Design
Crash Test Dummies

Deep Ecology
Design for Experiences & Services
Designing for Infrastructures
Discrimination
Diversity Axes

Ecofeminism
Emotion
Emotions in Design
Environment
Environmental justice
Environmental sustainability

fAIr – A Pensions Gap Start-up Initiative
Fairness
Feminism
First-Things-First-Manifesto

Gender fair iconic language
Gender Pay Gap
Gender Pay Gap in Tech

Intersectional Design Cards
Intersectionality
Intertemporal justice
Intervention Design

Manifesto for gender sensitive communication design
Marine science & Gender
Mobility

Norms

Petromasculinity
Product Design
Programming
Programming

Randi – A Concept for a Radically Inclusive Virtual Assistant

Savings Principle
Scripts
Social norms
Social Robots
Stereotypes
Sustainability
Sustainability Goals
Symbolic interactionism

Technology
The paradox of the stereotype

Virtual Assistance & Gender
Visual culture

Women in Tech Industry

Authors
(in order of appearance)

Julia-Constance Dissel
Julia is Professor for Practical Philosophy and Cultural Philosophy at University of Applied Sciences in Darmstadt, Germany as well as runs her own consultancy business for art & design projects. She was awarded Doctor of Philosophy in 2012 from Goethe University Frankfurt/M. after studying Philosophy, Art History and Archaeology in Frankfurt/M. and at the Albert-Ludwigs-University Freiburg and the University of Basel, Switzerland; additionally, she holds a postgraduate degree in Cultural and Media Practice from the Institute for German Literature and Didactic in Frankfurt/M. She has taught and researched in these fields at various academic institutions, amongst them the Max Planck Institute for European Legal History in Frankfurt/M., the faculty of Philosophy at the University of Oxford (UK), the HTWG Konstanz and The University of applied Sciences Darmstadt. She also was Visiting Professor for Perception Theory at the University of Arts and Design in Offenbach. Julia specialises in the field of Practical Philosophy and Art and Design Philosophy. Here she is most interested in the combination of empirical and philosophical findings in aesthetics and the interconnection of aesthetics and ethical dimensions. The feasibility of sustainability goals such as inclusion, diversity, and also ecological resource conservation, specifically in the context of design and technology has a growing influence on her teaching and thinking.

Melanie Levick-Parkin
Melanie Levick-Parkin is a feminist design educator and researcher, who is interested in how intersectional feminist approaches can create spaces where design can be ontologically remade and put into the service of futures that are materially more just for all planetary life. Her teaching and research explore how gendered power relations are materialised and incorporate visual communication, design & making practices in relation to intangible cultural heritage, heritage, and archaeology, informed by design-anthropological approaches. Having left the creative industry many years ago for a life in the academy, she has taught and led a wide range of design courses, including the PG Design Programme at Sheffield Hallam University, served as an External Examiner at many institutions - most recently for the Politecnico di Milano Doctoral school, supervises PHD research in relation to design for health; decolonising design; and ontological design, and

has contributed to a wide range of research and creative outputs which have included Horizon 2020 projects as well as collaborative exhibitions and public art in Greece and the USA. Her current focus in on ecofeminist philosophy and how it might further sharpen the feminist design lens in relation to 'more than human' design ontologies and futures.

Christian Bauer
Christian Bauer studied German philology, philosophy and political science in Würzburg and Cologne. He was awarded his doctorate with a thesis on the sacrificium intellectus in art at the University of Wuppertal in 2008 and has since taught art, design and media studies at various universities. He has been Professor of Design History and Design Theory at the Academy of Fine Arts (HBKsaar) in Saarbrücken since 2019. He has also been the Rector of HBKsaar since 2021. His research focuses on design ethics and ethical approaches in design history. To this end, he recently established the 'Institute for Design and Ethics'. The institute is currently focusing on scientific communication, research into anti-Semitism and issues of cultural sustainability, among other things. At the same time, as Rector of the HBKsaar and as a member of the Saarland Ministry of the Environment's team of experts, he promotes education for sustainable development.

Hannah Jones
Hannah Jones is a design educator and researcher with expertise in design, collaboration and sustainable futures. She currently supervises PhDs with a focus on metadesign (designing inclusive and participatory design processes) at University of Wales Trinity St. Davids, and teaches design research methods for the landscape architecture masters students at Greenwich University, London. She previously taught regularly at the Hasso Plattner Institute of Design (d.school), Stanford University, California, where she was a teaching fellow from 2015-2016. Her work at Stanford included developing intersectional approaches to designing socially and environmentally inclusive products and technologies.

Londa Schiebinger
Londa Schiebinger is the John L. Hinds Professor of History of Science in the History Department at Stanford University and Director of the EU/US Gendered Innovations in Science, Health & Medicine, Engineering, and Environment Project. From 2004-2010, Schiebinger served as the Director of Stanford's Clayman Institute for Gender Research. She is a member of the American Academy of Arts and Sciences. Schiebinger received her Ph.D. from Harvard University in 1984 and is a leading international authority on gender in science and technology. Over the past thirty years, Schiebinger's work has been devoted to teasing apart three analytically distinct but interlocking pieces of the gender and science puzzle: the history of women's participation in science; gender in the structure of scientific institutions; and the gendering of human knowledge. Londa Schiebin-

ger presented the keynote address and wrote the conceptual background paper for the United Nations' Expert Group Meeting on Gender, Science, and Technology, September 2010 in Paris. She presented the findings at the United Nations in New York, February 2011 with an update spring 2014. In 2022, she prepared the background paper for the United Nations 67th session of the Commission on the Status of Women's priority theme, Innovation and Technological Change, and Education in the Digital Age for Achieving Gender Equality and The Empowerment of all Women and Girls. Since 2023, Gendered Innovations has been a member of the UNFPA Equity 2030 Alliance.

Valeria Bucchetti
Valeria Bucchetti is Full Professor (Design Department of Politecnico di Milano); she was Chair BSc + MSc Communication Design (2018-2024). She teaches "Communication Design and Gender Culture" in the Design Master Degree. She is member of the Ph.D. Design board and she is member of the board of "Centro di Ricerca Interuniversitario Culture di Genere". She won the "Compasso d'Oro" Design Award (1998). Her research field concerns the theoretical aspects of identity systems and their communicative components and gender identities in the communication design domain, in which she has developed a great number of basic and applied research projects.

Francesca Casnati
Communication Designer, PhD. Her area of interest lies at the intersection of Communication Design, Gender Studies and Feminist Studies. Since 2018 she has been a member of the DCxCG – Communication Design for Gender Cultures – research group, at the Design Department, Politecnico di Milano and she cooperates with the Gender Cultures Interuniversity Research Centre. She teaches at the School of Design (Politecnico di Milano). She co-edited the publications 'We say stop. Contributi e riflessioni critiche per contrastare la violenza contro le donne' (2024) and 'Tracce di iper-in-visibilità.' (2022).

Franziska Beckert
Franziska Beckert holds a Master's degree in Project Management, Industrial Engineering, and Management from Beuth University of Applied Sciences Berlin, and a Bachelor's degree in Automotive Engineering from the Technical University Berlin. She further enriched her expertise with training in social justice and diversity at the University of Applied Sciences Potsdam. In 2018 she started working in the tech industry. Since 2022, she has been a Senior Product Manager at HeyJobs GmbH, where she leads strategic initiatives in Go-to-Market and Revenue Operations to enhance sales and marketing efficiency. Her commitment to gender diversity in the tech industry is evident through her published work with Budrich Academic Press, where she critically analyzed the underrepresentation of women in tech. She also participated as a panelist in discussions

on female empowerment in the tech industry, and has recorded a podcast episode on her publication.

Griselda Flesler
She is a graphic designer and holds a Master in Design Theory from University of Buenos Aires and she is a PhD candidate in social sciences. She is Principal Researcher and Director of the History, Archives, Gender and Affects Programme at the Institute of American Art and Aesthetic Research 'Mario J. Buschiazzo' (IAA- FADU-UBA) and Head Professor of Design and Gender Studies at FADU-University of Buenos Aires, also offering the PhD seminar 'Design e Gênero' (USP & UFMA, Brazil). Griselda is a Member of the International Gender Design Network (iGDN) and Coordinator of the Latin American Gender and Design Network (ReLaDyG). During 2022-2024 she was a member of the Advisory Board of the 'Diversity at the FHNW' Programme, Switzerland. She has been hired as co-Editor-in-Chief of Design and Culture Magazine, Taylor & Francis, USA, from 2026.
griselda.flesler@fadu.uba.ar

Carolina Spataro
Carolina Spartaro PhD in Social Sciences, master's in Communications and Culture, bachelor's in Communications (UBA). CONICET researcher at the Gino Germani Research Institute, University of Buenos Aires. Her research topics are the feminist tide in universities: resistance, support and ways of appropriation of the institutionalization processes of gender policies in higher education. Former Vice-Secretary of the Office of Gender at the School of Social Sciences at University of Buenos Aires. Extensive experience in the development and implementation of qualitative research projects and management work in the public and private sector. Experience in team coordination, training and evaluation tasks. carolinaspataro@yahoo.com.ar

Julia Pierzina
born in 1991, studied Media Art and Design in Saarbrücken and Aix-en-Provence and researched gender perceptions of young people in the context of school in her dissertation. 2025 Dr. Phil. at HBK Saar. As an intervention designer at K8 Institute for Strategic Aesthetics, she focuses on gender equity in digitalization and transformation processes with new technologies. Pierzina is a board member of the international Gender Design Network and was a jury member of the iphiGenia Gender Design Award 2023.